This book traces the origins, and provides the most complete account, of the insurgency that has racked the Indian-controlled portion (about two-thirds) of Jammu and Kashmir since 1989. The first theoretically grounded account, it is based on extensive interviews with government officials, Kashmiri activists, journalists, members of nongovernmental organizations, and military personnel in India, Pakistan, and the United States.

Ganguly's central argument is that the insurgency can be explained by the linked processes of political mobilization and institutional decay. In an attempt to woo the citizens of India's only Muslim-majority state, the national government in New Delhi dramatically helped expand literacy, mass media, and higher education in Jammu and Kashmir. These processes produced a generation of politically knowledgeable and sophisticated Kashmiris. Simultaneously, the national government, fearful of potential secessionist proclivities among the Kashmiris, systematically stultified the development of political institutions in the state. Unable to express dissent in an institutional context, this new generation of Kashmiris resorted to violence.

WOODROW WILSON CENTER SERIES

The crisis in Kashmir

Other books in the series

Michael J. Lacey, editor, *Religion and Twentieth-Century American Intellectual Life*

Michael J. Lacey, editor, *The Truman Presidency*

Joseph Kruzel and Michael H. Haltzel, editors, *Between the Blocs: Problems and Prospects for Europe's Neutral and Nonaligned States*

William C. Brumfield, editor, *Reshaping Russian Architecture: Western Technology, Utopian Dreams*

Mark N. Katz, editor, *The USSR and Marxist Revolutions in the Third World*

Walter Reich, editor, *Origins of Terrorism: Psychologies, Ideologies, Theologies, States of Mind*

Mary O. Furner and Barry Supple, editors, *The State and Economic Knowledge: The American and British Experiences*

Michael J. Lacey and Knud Haakonssen, editors, *A Culture of Rights: The Bill of Rights in Philosophy, Politics, and Law—1791 and 1991*

Robert J. Donovan and Ray Scherer, *Unsilent Revolution: Television News and American Public Life, 1948–1991*

Nelson Lichtenstein and Howell John Harris, editors, *Industrial Democracy in America: The Ambiguous Promise*

William Craft Brumfield and Blair A. Ruble, editors, *Russian Housing in the Modern Age: Design and Social History*

Michael J. Lacey and Mary O. Furner, editors, *The State and Social Investigation in Britain and the United States*

Hugh Ragsdale, editor and translator, *Imperial Russian Foreign Policy*

Dermot Keogh and Michael H. Haltzel, editors, *Northern Ireland and the Politics of Reconciliation*

Joseph Klaits and Michael H. Haltzel, editors, *The Global Ramifications of the French Revolution*

René Lemarchand, *Burundi: Ethnocide as Discourse and Practice*

James R. Millar and Sharon L. Wolchik, editors, *The Social Legacy of Communism*

James M. Morris, editor, *On Mozart*

Continued on page following index

The crisis in Kashmir

Portents of war, hopes of peace

Šumit Ganguly

WOODROW WILSON CENTER PRESS

AND

CAMBRIDGE
UNIVERSITY PRESS

PUBLISHED BY THE PRESS SYNDICATE OF THE UNIVERSITY OF CAMBRIDGE
The Pitt Building, Trumpington Street, Cambridge CB2 1RP, United Kingdom
and
THE WOODROW WILSON CENTER PRESS

CAMBRIDGE UNIVERSITY PRESS
The Edinburgh Building, Cambridge CB2 2RU, United Kingdom
40 West 20th Street, New York, NY 10011-4211, USA
10 Stamford Road, Oakleigh, Melbourne 3166, Australia

© Šumit Ganguly 1997

First published 1997

Printed in the United States of America

Typeset in Sabon

A catalog record for this book is available from the British Library.

Library of Congress Cataloging-in-Publication Data
Ganguly, Šumit.
The Crisis in Kashmir: portents of war, hopes of peace / Šumit
Ganguly.
p.   cm. — (Woodrow Wilson Center series)
Includes bibliographical references and index.
ISBN 0-521-59066-3
1. Jammu and Kashmir (India)—Politics and government.   I. Title.
II. Series.
DS485.K27G37   1997
954'.6—dc21   96-39401
CIP

ISBN 0-521-59066-3 hardback

WOODROW WILSON CENTER PRESS

The Woodrow Wilson Center Press publishes books written in substantial part at the Center or otherwise prepared under its sponsorship by fellows, guest scholars, staff members, and other program participants. Conclusions or opinions expressed in Center publications and programs are those of the authors and speakers and do not necessarily reflect the views of the Center staff, fellows, trustees, advisory groups, or any individuals or organizations that provide financial support to the Center.

Woodrow Wilson Center Press
Editorial Offices
370 L'Enfant Promenade, S.W., Suite 704
Washington, D.C. 20024-2518
telephone: (202) 287-3000, ext. 218

To Stephen P. Cohen and Robert L. Hardgrave, Jr.—
teachers, supporters, and friends

Contents

Acknowledgments

Writing a book on an insurgency entails reliance on a spectrum of sources. Some of these sources, understandably, wish to remain anonymous. As much as I would like to acknowledge the contributions of many individuals in India, Pakistan, and the United States, I must respect their preference for anonymity.

Friends and colleagues around the globe provided me with support, assistance, advice, and encouragement. They all have made the task of writing this book substantially easier. I owe particular thanks to Ray Andrews, Steve Coll, Barbara Crossette, Stephen Dale, David Magier, Neelam Deo, Robert L. Hardgrave, Jr., Selig Harrison, Harold Gould, Col. David Smith, Gautam Adhikari, Kanti Bajpai, Maj. Gen. Dipankar Banerjee, Harinder Baweja, Pran Chopra, Sunil Dasgupta, Edward Desmond, Anupam Dhar, Mirwaiz Omar Farooq, Madhukar Gupta, Ved Marwah, Hamish McDonald, the late Dilip Mukherjee, Ashok Jaitley, Ashok Kantha, Surjit Singh Oberoi, Philip Oldenburg, Riyaz Punjabi, Balraj Puri, Jairam Ramesh, Ram Mohan Rao, Governor Girish Saxena, Bhabani Sen Gupta, Saifuddin Soz, Air Commodore Jasjit Singh, K. Subrahmanyam, Phillips Talbot, B. G. Verghese, Raziullah Azmi, Hasan-Askari Rizvi, Shafquat Kakakhel, Tapan Raychaudhuri, and Subrata Kumar Mitra.

I also wish to acknowledge the extraordinary support of the staff of the Woodrow Wilson International Center for Scholars in Washington, D.C. We are unfortunately living in an era when it is popularly believed that all government support for intellectual endeavors is of questionable merit. My year at the Woodrow Wilson Center certainly belied that assumption. My fellowship there in 1993–4 provided an unparalleled milieu for intellectual endeavor; without that year, this book would not have materialized for another ten years. Three persons merit particular mention: Charles Blitzer, director of the Woodrow Wilson Center; Mary Brown Bullock, former director of the Center's Asia Program; and Joseph Brinley, director of the Woodrow Wilson Center Press. And while at the Center, I was privileged to have a research assistant of the intellectual caliber, endless energy, and boundless good cheer of Shamsuddin Mahmud.

I thank also the Professional Staff Congress of the City University of New York for providing two grants for field research and travel, and the United States Institute of Peace for preliminary research support.

Amitabh Mattoo and Leo Rose carefully read this book in manuscript form and saved me from a number of potential pitfalls. Stephen P. Cohen and Jack Snyder both painstakingly read the manuscript at an early stage and provided important substantive and theoretical insights. Wajahat Habibullah unstintingly shared with me his extensive knowledge of Kashmir.

Finally, I thank my wife, Traci Nagle, who read through endless drafts of this manuscript, shaped it substantively and stylistically, and cheerfully tolerated my obsession with Kashmir. Without her support and encouragement, none of this would have happened.

Despite the efforts of all these people, some errors may persist. They are, of course, all mine.

Introduction

This book is an attempt to trace the roots of the insurgency in the portion of Kashmir that is juridically deemed to be a part of India. It also examines what might be done to manage and even resolve the insurgency.

My interest in Kashmir stems from a long-standing concern with ethnic mobilization, the relationship between domestic and external conflicts, and political violence in South Asia. The insurgency raises questions about managing ethnic tensions in a poly-ethnic, plural, democratic, and secular state. The manner in which the unrest in Kashmir is eventually handled will have vitally important effects on two of the most significant features of the Indian polity, namely, democracy and secularism.

This study is also important from the standpoint of larger, theoretical considerations. The "first wave" of modernization scholarship, which was profoundly influenced by Weberian ideas, postulated the declining significance of ethnicity, contending that it was a remnant of traditional societies. The "second wave" of scholarship not only challenged such notions but also pointed out how traditional forms of social organization might successfully adapt to modern forms.[1] Other scholars pointed to the difficulties of fashioning nation-states out of "old societies and new states."[2] Still others developed taxonomic explanations for ethnic mobiliza-

---

[1] Samuel P. Huntington, *Political Order in Changing Societies* (New Haven: Yale University Press, 1968); Lloyd I. Rudolph and Susanne Hoeber Rudolph, *The Modernity of Tradition* (Chicago: University of Chicago Press, 1967).

[2] Clifford Geertz, *The Interpretation of Cultures* (New York: Basic Books, 1973).

tion.[3] One scholar drew a useful dichotomy between "primordial" and "instrumental" bases of ethnic mobilization.[4] Yet there is a paucity of sound, theoretically informed literature on specific cases of ethnic separatism.[5] My hope in writing this book on the Kashmir dispute is that a study explicitly guided by theoretical premises may help our understanding of Kashmir and, at the same time, refine current thinking on ethnic separatism. In bridging international relations and comparative politics, this book is also intended to expand the existing theoretical and case-study literature on ethnonationalism, irredentism, and international relations, literature that is currently extraordinarily slim.[6]

My initial work on Kashmir was an attempt to trace the origins of the Kashmir dispute to the process of British colonial withdrawal; the differing ideological commitments of the two principal nationalist parties, the Congress and the Muslim League; and the subsequent Pakistani irredentist claim on Kashmir.[7] I concluded, after my study of the three Indo-Pakistani wars, that conflict was most likely when the ideological commitments that formed the basis of the two states started to disintegrate. In a related article I explored in more detail the origins of the 1965 war over Kashmir.[8] I argued

---

[3] Joseph Rothschild, *Ethnopolitics* (New York: Columbia University Press, 1981).

[4] Crawford Young, "The Temple of Ethnicity," *World Politics* 35:4 (July 1983): 652–62.

[5] One important exception is Frederick L. Shiels, *Ethnic Separatism in World Politics* (Lanham, Md.: University Press of America, 1984).

[6] Astre Sukhre and Lela Garner Noble, *Ethnic Conflict in International Politics* (New York: Praeger, 1978); Eric J. Hobsbawm, *Nations and Nationalism since 1780* (Cambridge: Cambridge University Press, 1990); John Mayall, *Nationalism and International Society* (Cambridge: Cambridge University Press, 1990); Naomi Chazan, ed., *Irredentism and International Politics* (Boulder: Lynne Reinner, 1991).

[7] Šumit Ganguly, *The Origins of War in South Asia: The Indo-Pakistani Conflicts since 1947*, 2d ed. (Boulder: Westview, 1994).

[8] Šumit Ganguly, "Avoiding War in Kashmir," *Foreign Affairs* 69:5 (Winter 1990/1991): 57–73.

that the apparent threats to India's secular credo following Jawaharlal Nehru's death, manifested in anti-Indian agitations in the Kashmir valley, reinforced Pakistani irredentism and led to the second Kashmir war. But in both cases I failed to anticipate the renewal of ethnic mobilization in Kashmir. In fact, I contended that although some ethnic and separatist sentiment did exist in Kashmir, it was not likely to expand significantly in the future.[9]

In this book, I shall explore three dimensions of the insurgency in Kashmir. First, I shall deal with the process of ethnic mobilization and the emergence of Kashmiri separatism in the 1980s. As I have argued elsewhere, I believe that the rise of separatist sentiment in Kashmir, as well as in other portions of India, is part of the second wave of ethnolinguistic assertion.[10] The first wave was concerned with the creation of linguistically based states under the aegis of the States Reorganization Act of 1956. The long-term survival of the Indian state depends on its ability to reaffirm its commitments to secularism. It must also fashion a new compact with the recently mobilized minorities, one that will accommodate their demands for political participation and social justice. How will this be accomplished? What strategies will be adopted, leading to what new political practices and arrangements?

Second, I shall examine the bilateral dimensions of the Kashmir crisis. Pakistan's irredentist claim to Kashmir has led some of its key decision-makers to provide support to the insurgency. Although this is understandable, it could entail substantial costs for Pakistan in the longer term. Most dangerously, India may pursue a similar strategy in the Pakistani province of Sind, where there is considerable disaffection with the Punjabi-dominated Pakistani regime.

Third, I shall relate this case to the larger body of literature on ethnonationalism. A widely accepted hypothesis in this literature

---

[9] Ganguly, *Origins of War.*
[10] Ganguly, "Avoiding War in Kashmir"; Šumit Ganguly and Kanti P. Bajpai, "India and the Crisis in Kashmir," *Asian Survey* 34:5 (May 1994): 401–16.

suggests that differential rates of modernization in ethnically plural societies frequently ignite ethnic conflict. Modernization offers the possibility of socioeconomic mobility and threatens long-existing bonds of kith, kin, and community.[11] In the Kashmir case, I shall argue, modernization exposed young Kashmiris to the possibilities of alternative futures, but the political process largely choked off such opportunities. With democratic dissent curbed, violent and separatist sentiments came to the fore. I shall be concerned here with why the asymmetry between mobilization and accommodation caused disaffected Kashmiris to take an ethnic and violent turn.

Writing this book on Kashmir has proved to be a revealing experience from both personal and scholarly standpoints. From a personal standpoint, it brought home the extraordinary dangers of conducting research on an area racked by violence and unrest. Informants, ranging from journalists covering the insurgency to political leaders with connections to the insurgents, were often wary of speaking with an American professor of Indian origin. Yet many of them overcame their misgivings to share a trove of information and analysis. Government officials were on some occasions exceedingly forthcoming and candid and on other occasions extremely reticent and downright disingenuous.

Two issues encountered in this research enterprise are particularly noteworthy. First, reliable statistical information in the public domain, although it may putatively be unclassified, is virtually impossible to obtain, whether in the United States or in India. Consequently, lacunae remain in building accurate statistical portraits of particular themes. These gaps should be filled as time passes.

Second, although my intellectual moorings remain firmly entrenched in the canons of positivist social science, on occasion I wish that I were an adherent of postmodernism. In the course of

---

[11] Myron Weiner, *Sons of the Soil: Migration and Ethnic Conflict in India* (Princeton: Princeton University Press, 1978).

my research, I found that seemingly reliable accounts of specific incidents frequently turned out to be wildly inaccurate and partisan. Eventually, only multiple attempts at reconstructing events yielded what I hope is a reasonably accurate picture of what transpired.

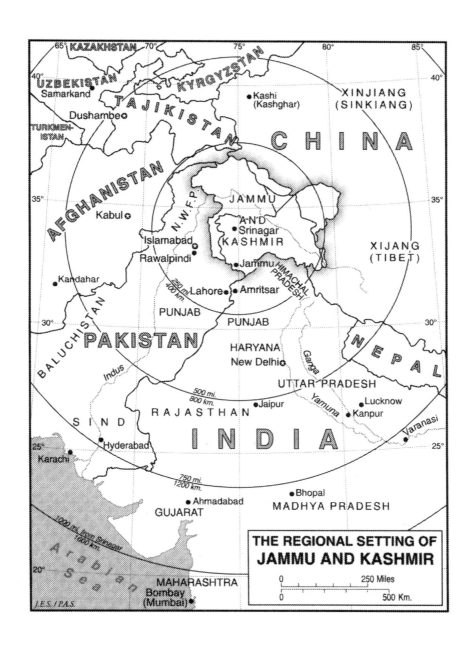

THE REGIONAL SETTING OF
JAMMU AND KASHMIR

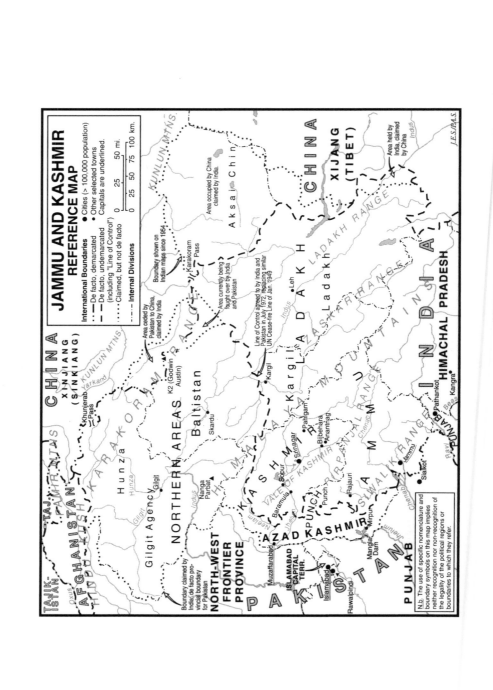

1

The Kashmir conundrum

In 1989 a violent separatist movement erupted in the fabled Indian state of Jammu and Kashmir. Several months of sporadic strikes, demonstrations, and other antigovernment activities peaked in December 1989 with the kidnapping of the daughter of the Indian minister for home affairs. The secessionist agenda that a small coterie of underground organizations had been promoting for decades suddenly seemed to evoke widespread popular support. Buoyed by the antigovernment sentiment that had been building over the latter half of the 1980s, the Jammu and Kashmir Liberation Front (JKLF) and other, less organized secessionist groups mounted a campaign of violence against the Indian state.

Faced with this relatively sudden burst of ethnoreligious and secessionist violence, the government deployed security forces, including units of the Indian Army, the Border Security Forces (BSF), the Central Reserve Police Force (CRPF), the Indo-Tibetan Border Police (ITBP), and most recently, the Rashtriya Rifles (special units of the Indian Army trained in counterinsurgency activities), in an attempt to quell the insurgency. Assessments of the number of Indian security personnel deployed in the Kashmir valley, the locus of the insurgency, place the total near four hundred thousand.[1]

---

[1] The highest figure that has been suggested is around half a million. But most reliable estimates place the figure around four hundred thousand. See Anthony Davis, "The Conflict in Kashmir," *Jane's Intelligence Review* 7:1 (1995): 40.

The deployment in Kashmir is India's largest and most significant counterinsurgency operation to date.

The operation has proved enormously costly to the Indian exchequer. Because of the intricacies of national budgetary allocations, precise estimates are unavailable. Nevertheless, educated estimates suggest that nearly 60 percent of the annual administrative expenses of the state of Jammu and Kashmir are now devoted to security-related activities.[2] The insurgency has also taken its human toll. During its first six years, this conflict claimed more than fifteen thousand insurgents, security personnel, hostages, and bystanders. In addition, some two hundred thousand, primarily Hindu Kashmiris, have fled homes and businesses in the valley and are living as refugees in Jammu and elsewhere in India.[3]

Not since the state's troubled integration into India in 1947 has Kashmir or India witnessed such an uprising. Granted, separatist sentiment has long existed in Kashmir, and popular and sometimes even violent protests have taken place there, particularly in 1963. And many other regions of India have seen violent uprisings along class, ethnoreligious, and ethnolinguistic lines since independence.[4] But none of these other incidents captured the imaginations of or actively involved such large segments of the population, nor did they entail such human and material losses as the current insurgency in Kashmir.[5]

Nor has any other internal discord in India seemed so impervious to resolution. Indeed, with the possible exceptions of the Anglo-Irish, the Greek-Turkish-Cypriot, and the Israeli-

[2] Author interview with senior Indian government official, August 1995.

[3] For estimates of the number of Kashmiris who have fled the valley, see Kanhya L. Kaul and M. K. Teng, "Human Rights Violations of Kashmiri Hindus," in *Perspectives on Kashmir: The Roots of Conflict in South Asia,* ed. Raju G. C. Thomas (Boulder: Westview, 1992), 176, and Robert G. Wirsing, *India, Pakistan, and the Kashmir Dispute: On Regional Conflict and Its Resolution* (New York: St. Martin's, 1994), 126.

[4] For an early, trenchant, if somewhat alarmist treatment of these movements, see Selig Harrison, *India: The Most Dangerous Decades* (Princeton: Princeton University Press, 1960).

[5] On this point, see Jyoti Bhusan Das Gupta, *Jammu and Kashmir* (The Hague: Martinus Nijhoff, 1968).

Palestinian disputes, few conflicts in the post–World War II era have proved as intractable as the fifty-year Indo-Pakistani argument over Kashmir, one that has been rejuvenated by the current insurgency.

Yet the present incarnation of the Kashmir conflict, official Indian pronouncements notwithstanding, is significantly different from its previous manifestations. The conflict in its earlier form, which led to two wars between India and Pakistan in 1947–8 and 1965, was strictly bilateral; the source of discord stemmed from India's formal claim to the entire state of Jammu and Kashmir and from Pakistan's irredentist claim to the Indian-held portion of Kashmir.[6] The peoples of either Pakistani-held "Azad Kashmir" (literally "Free Kashmir") or Indian-held Kashmir were not active participants in the bilateral conflicts. Indeed, in 1965 Kashmiris in the valley were principally responsible for unraveling a carefully knit Pakistani strategy of infiltration aimed at forcibly seizing the Indian-held portion of Kashmir. Today, the situation exists in exactly the reverse; both expatriate Kashmiris within Pakistan and the vast majority of the residents of the Kashmir valley are, to varying degrees, active participants in the conflict.

The scale and the intensity of the conflict, along with the conditions of the use of force against the insurgents, have focused international attention on Kashmir. Both Indian and international human rights groups have criticized the excessive and unauthorized use of force by the security forces, particularly the BSF.[7] Charges have repeatedly been exchanged between Islamabad and New Delhi: the former accusing India of widespread repression in

---

[6] For a detailed analysis and comparison of the three Indo-Pakistani conflicts, see Šumit Ganguly, *The Origins of War in South Asia: The Indo-Pakistani Conflicts since 1947,* 2d ed. (Boulder: Westview, 1994).

[7] For an Indian critique, see Tapan Bose, Dinesh Mohan, Gautam Navlakha, and Sumanto Banerjee, "India's Kashmir War," in Asghar Ali Engineer, ed., *Secular Crown on Fire: The Kashmir Problem* (Delhi: Ajanta, 1991). For international critiques of the human rights situation, see Asia Watch and Physicians for Human Rights, *The Human Rights Crisis in Kashmir: A Pattern of Impunity* (New York: Asia Watch, A Division of Human Rights Watch, 1993).

Kashmir, the latter accusing Pakistan of aiding and abetting the insurgents. Finally, external powers, principally the United States, have expressed concerns about the potential spillover of the conflict. U.S. officials have articulated fears of an Indo-Pakistani conflict that could escalate to the nuclear level.[8]

Such misgivings, though exaggerated, are not entirely groundless. India and Pakistan have resorted to war three times since the British colonial disengagement from the subcontinent in 1947.[9] Two of these wars, those of 1947–8 and 1965, were fought directly over Pakistan's irredentist claim to Kashmir.[10] More recently, there have been at least two "war scares," in 1987 and 1990.[11] Most important, despite persistent official denials, both India and Pakistan are incipient nuclear weapons states. Their possession of nuclear weapons has spawned an important debate about the prospects of stability and instability in the subcontinent.[12] The potential renewal

[8] See testimony of James Woolsey before the Senate Committee on Governmental Affairs, *Hearing on Proliferation Threats of the 1990s*, 103d Cong., 1st sess., February 24, 1993 (Washington, D.C.: U.S. Government Printing Office, 1993).

[9] See Ganguly, *Origins of War*, and Šumit Ganguly, "Wars without End? The Indo-Pakistani Conflict," *Annals of the American Academy of Political and Social Science* 541 (September 1995): 167–78.

[10] Myron Weiner, "The Macedonian Syndrome," *World Politics* 23:4 (July 1971): 665–83.

[11] On the 1987 "Brasstacks" crisis, see Kanti Bajpai, P. R. Chari, Pervaiz Iqbal Cheema, Stephen P. Cohen, and Šumit Ganguly, *Brasstacks and Beyond: Perception and the Management of Crisis in South Asia* (New Delhi: Manohar, 1995). For a thoughtful analysis of the 1990 crisis, see Devin T. Hagerty, "The Theory and Practice of Nuclear Deterrence in South Asia" (Ph.D. diss., University of Pennsylvania, 1995).

[12] Whether the incipient nuclearization of the subcontinent has brought about greater stability or has enhanced the dangers of war is the subject of an important debate. For a general discussion of the arguments on both sides, see Scott D. Sagan and Kenneth N. Waltz, *The Spread of Nuclear Weapons: A Debate* (New York: W. W. Norton, 1994). For a more specific view of the arguments as they pertain to South Asia, see Šumit Ganguly, "Emergent Security Issues in South Asia," in *Director's Series on Proliferation*, no. 8, ed. Kathleen C. Bailey (Livermore, Calif.: Lawrence Livermore National Laboratory, 1995).

of bilateral conflict between India and Pakistan has again focused a degree of international attention on the region and on the crisis in Kashmir itself.

The issue of Kashmir is now virtually inseparable from Indo-Pakistani bilateral relations. Though some of the roots of the crisis are indigenous, systematic Pakistani involvement in and support for the insurgency have dramatically affected Indo-Pakistani relations. The resolution of the crisis will require a two-pronged approach: between India and Pakistan, bilateral talks designed to end Pakistan's support for the insurgency and at the same time to end Pakistan's irredentist claim on Kashmir; and among the various insurgent groups, internal reform and negotiations intended to bring about a degree of peace and normalcy within Jammu and Kashmir.

Little progress can be made in Indo-Pakistani relations unless the insurgency in Kashmir is resolved. As long as violence and instability continue to rack the Kashmir valley and as long as Indian security forces are present there in substantial numbers, the Kashmir issue will remain a live wire in Pakistani domestic politics. Until the issue is resolved, therefore, Pakistani politicians will use the Kashmir issue as a soapbox from which to rail against any sort of rapprochement with India over the territorial dispute. Simultaneously, within India, those opposed to improving relations with Pakistan will dwell on Pakistan's complicity in the insurgency.

From the history of the last six years it is clear that simple force will not bring an easy end to the insurgency. The solution to the problem must address the underlying grievances of the population, particularly in the valley. First, some fundamental questions must be answered. What are the origins of this ethnoreligious, secessionist movement? Why did it emerge in the late 1980s in particular? What explains the responses of the Indian state to the insurgency? What, if any, is the larger significance of the insurgency for the integrity of the Indian state? What are the prospects of conflict resolution? These are the five central questions that shape this book.

THE PALIMPSEST OF THE PAST

The origins of the present conflict cannot be grasped without some understanding of the history of the region. In 1947, at the time of the independence and partition of the British Indian empire, Kashmir, like 561 other so-called princely states, was notionally independent as long as the rulers recognized the "paramountcy" of the British Crown. In effect, the rulers of the princely states were autonomous except in three vital spheres: defense, foreign affairs, and communications. Kashmir, though predominantly Muslim (75 percent of the population at the time of independence and partition), had a Hindu monarch, Maharaja Hari Singh.

The Hindu monarchy in Kashmir had been established in 1846. The British had granted Maharaja Gulab Singh of Lahore domain over Kashmir for the paltry sum of 7.5 million rupees. The maharaja was given this bargain kingdom for two reasons. First, he had assisted the British in making an orderly retreat from the disastrous British Afghan expedition. Second, at the conclusion of the Anglo-Sikh war of 1845 and the defeat of the Lahore kingdom, Gulab Singh had indicated that he would protect British interests in the Punjab.[13]

In light of the prevailing standards of the day, Maharaja Gulab Singh's rule in Kashmir was reasonably enlightened. His predominantly Muslim subjects were not treated any worse than their Hindu counterparts. His successors, however, proved to be less open-minded. As a consequence of government service the Kashmiri Brahmins, known as "pandits," and the Dogras came to control most of the choice agricultural lands. The majority of the Muslim population who worked on these lands were subject to the pandits and the Dogras.

The last Hindu monarch of Kashmir, Maharaja Hari Singh, did little to improve the plight of his Muslim subjects. Ian Copland has succinctly summarized the situation of the Muslim community in the state:

[13] Rajesh Kadian, *The Kashmir Tangle: Issues and Options* (Boulder: Westview, 1993).

Though they comprised 53 per cent of the population in the southern, or Jammu province, and upwards of 93 per cent in the more populous northern, or Kashmir province, the Muslims were a community without wealth or influence. At the policy-making level, power was shared between the dynastic ruler Maharaja Hari Singh and a four-man executive council, which in 1931 consisted of the Maharaja's brother, two British officers loaned by the Government of India, and a Sikh. In the bureaucracy, Hindus and Sikhs held 78 per cent of gazetted appointments compared to the Muslims' 22 per cent. At the local government level the disparity was less marked overall but non-Muslims still dominated, especially in Jammu: for instance, the Tehsildars of Kotli and Rajouri, the Naib Tehsildars of Bhimber, Naoshera, Kotli and Rajouri, the Superintendent and Deputy-Superintendent of Police at Kotli and "nearly all the Magistrates" were either Sikhs or Hindus, while in Mirpur Tehsil it was estimated that 94 per cent of *patwaris* (village record-keepers) were Kashmiri Brahmins.[14]

During the maharaja's tenure, opposition to his rule coalesced under the leadership of a charismatic young Kashmiri Muslim, Sheikh Mohammed Abdullah. Abdullah founded a political party, the All Jammu and Kashmir Muslim Conference, in 1932. Later, under the influence of another prominent Kashmiri pandit, Jawaharlal Nehru (who was to become India's first prime minister), Abdullah nominally and substantively altered the orientation of his party. By changing the party's name in 1939 to the All Jammu and Kashmir National Conference, Abdullah effectively dispensed with the communal tenor that had been associated with the previous name of the party. Substantively, he sought to collaborate with Kashmiri Hindus, including the noted local journalist and political activist Prem Nath Bazaz. Abdullah's opposition to the maharaja's rule led to his incarceration during the Second World War. His imprisonment did little to undermine the strength of the movement, however. Instead, the two principal stalwarts of the Indian nationalist movement, Jawaharlal Nehru and Mohandas Gandhi, rallied to Sheikh Abdullah's cause. The opposition to the

---

[14] Ian Copland, "Islam and Political Mobilization in Kashmir, 1931–34," *Pacific Affairs* 54:2 (Summer 1981): 233–4.

maharaja's rule in Kashmir became enmeshed with the larger cause of India's independence from the United Kingdom.

THE CONTESTED ACCESSION

The dispute over the accession of Kashmir to India can be traced to the profoundly divergent conceptions of nation-building that underlay the Indian and Pakistani nationalist movements. The Indian National Congress, which spearheaded the Indian nationalist movement, was committed to the notion of creating a secular and democratic state. The Pakistani nationalist movement, in contrast, sought to create a religiously based state that would serve as a homeland for South Asian Muslims.[15] Possession of Kashmir, a Muslim-majority state abutting the two nascent states, therefore assumed a significance far greater than a mere territorial claim. For Indian nationalists such as Nehru, the integration of Kashmir into India was critical because it would demonstrate that all faiths could live under the aegis of a secular state. By the same token, Pakistani nationalists such as Mohammed Ali Jinnah saw the absorption of Kashmir into Pakistan as equally critical, but for diametrically opposite reasons. For Jinnah, Pakistan would be "incomplete" without Kashmir. In essence, Pakistan's claim to Kashmir was and remains irredentist.[16]

In the weeks and months preceding the independence and partition of the British Indian empire, Lord Mountbatten, the last viceroy, made it clear that the doctrine of paramountcy would lapse after British withdrawal. The rulers of the princely states, in effect, had two choices: They could join one or the other of the two emergent states, India or Pakistan. Under the terms of the Indian Independence Act, none of the princely states would be allowed to declare independence. Two qualifications were added to Mount-

---

[15] The literature on this subject is voluminous. The most succinct statement about the structures, ideologies, and mobilization strategies of the two nationalist movements can be found in Paul Brass, *Language, Religion, and Politics in North India* (Cambridge: Cambridge University Press, 1974).

[16] See Weiner, "The Macedonian Syndrome."

batten's directive on the lapse of paramountcy. First, he stated that certain "geographical compulsions" would have to be kept in mind, to provide the emergent states with somewhat contiguous territories.[17] Consequently, the nawab of Khairpur, in Sind, and the nizam of Hyderabad, in southern India, were forced by geography to accede to Pakistan and India, respectively.[18] Second, states that were predominantly Hindu would go to India while those that were predominantly Muslim would go to Pakistan.

Yet despite the seeming simplicity of these principles, in fact they were neither simple nor easily implemented.[19] Kashmir posed a particular problem. As mentioned earlier, it had a predominantly Muslim population and a Hindu monarch. Moreover, it abutted *both* the emerging states—India and Pakistan.

To add to the dilemma of accession, the ruler of Kashmir, Maharaja Hari Singh, harbored visions of independence, despite Mountbatten's explicit injunction and despite entreaties from both Indian and Pakistani representatives. Accordingly, he temporized on the issue of accession, even after the granting of independence to India and Pakistan in August 1947. During the first week of October 1947, a tribal rebellion broke out near Poonch, in the northwestern reaches of Kashmir. Pakistani troops, disguised as local tribesmen, quickly joined the rebels.[20] On the morning of October 22 the invading column, composed of Pathans (members

[17] As quoted in C. H. Philips, *The Evolution of India and Pakistan* (London: Oxford University Press, 1962), 438.

[18] The Indian "police action" against Hyderabad left the nizam little choice but to accede to India. On this point, see Ganguly, *Origins of War.*

[19] A wealth of literature exists on this subject. The best statement from the British standpoint is probably H. V. Hodson, *The Great Divide: Britain-India-Pakistan* (Karachi: Oxford University Press, 1985). The best statement of the Pakistani position can be obtained from Chaudhuri Mohammed Ali, *The Emergence of Pakistan* (New York: Columbia University Press, 1967). The Indian position is spelled out in V. P. Menon, *The Story of the Integration of the Indian States* (Madras: Orient Longman, 1961).

[20] The best evidence of Pakistan's involvement in support of the uprising can be found in Major General Akbar Khan, *Raiders in Kashmir* (Karachi: Pak Publishers, 1970), and Hodson, *The Great Divide.* For an argument that contends that the uprising was less than spontaneous, see Prem Shankar Jha, *Kashmir, 1947: Rival Versions of History* (Delhi: Oxford University Press, 1996).

of a tribal group from the North West Frontier Province of Pakistan) and regular Pakistani army personnel in mufti, captured the town of Muzaffarabad. The majority of the Muslim troops in the Jammu and Kashmir State Forces stationed in Muzaffarabad joined the raiders and massacred their Dogra (Hindu) counterparts.[21] After engaging in mayhem and rapine in Muzaffarabad, they headed toward Srinagar, the capital of Kashmir.

Caught in a panic, Hari Singh initially appealed to the neighboring princely state of Patiala for assistance. The maharaja of Patiala sent him an infantry battalion from the Patiala State Forces, but this unit proved inadequate to the task at hand.[22] Faced with the imminent fall of Srinagar, Maharaja Hari Singh then appealed to Lord Mountbatten for assistance. Mountbatten received this request on October 24 and called a meeting of the Indian Defence Committee the next morning. In consultation with Prime Minister Nehru and Home Minister Sardar Vallabhbhai Patel, Mountbatten decided that Indian troops could be sent only after the maharaja signed the Instrument of Accession. He inserted an important caveat, however, with which Nehru promptly concurred: The people of Kashmir would have to ratify the accession. Given the prevailing chaos, this effort had to be deferred until normalcy was restored. In the interim, Nehru agreed that he would accept the support of Sheikh Mohammed Abdullah in lieu of a popular ratification.[23]

The same day (October 25), V. P. Menon was dispatched to Srinagar to advise Maharajah Hari Singh to sign the Instrument of Accession in order to obtain Indian military assistance. Menon

[21] Major General Lionel Protip Sen, *Slender Was the Thread: Kashmir Confrontation, 1947–48* (Bombay: Orient Longmans, 1969), 36–37.

[22] Prem Shankar Jha contends that the Patiala troops may have been sent without either the knowledge or the consent of the government of India. On this point, see Jha, *Kashmir, 1947,* 59–61.

[23] See Hodson, *The Great Divide,* 449, and Richard Sisson and Leo Rose, *War and Secession* (Berkeley: University of California Press, 1991). The accession to India was provisional in that both parties agreed to subsequently hold a plebiscite after normalcy had been restored and the invaders repulsed from Kashmir. See Appendix 1 for the text of the Instrument of Accession.

returned to New Delhi on the next day with the signed instrument and the maharajah's request for Indian troops. On October 27, Lord Mountbatten accepted the Instrument of Accession. Shortly thereafter, Indian paratroopers landed in Srinagar.[24]

Despite the quick dispatch of the Indian troops to Srinagar, the invaders managed to occupy approximately one-third of the state. Full-scale fighting between Indian and Pakistani regular forces broke out in November 1947.[25] Neither side made significant territorial gains throughout the month of December, and the fighting continued in a desultory fashion. With no quick resolution in sight, at the suggestion of Lord Mountbatten on December 20, 1947, the Indian cabinet decided to refer the case to the UN Security Council. Accordingly, a complaint was lodged to the council on January 1, 1948.

In the ensuing years, some controversy has arisen about the legality of the accession of Kashmir to India. These questions are tendentious and must be addressed. Much of the argument is based upon highly prejudicial inferences and little or no evidence.[26] The best evidence of the legality of the accession, of Pakistan's complicity in provoking the tribal rebellion, and of

[24] Vernon Hewitt, *Reclaiming the Past: The Search for Political and Cultural Unity in Contemporary Kashmir* (London: Portland Books, 1995).

[25] The best account of the war, albeit from the Indian perspective, can be found in Sen, *Slender Was the Thread*.

[26] The most direct challenge has come from Alistair Lamb, *Kashmir: A Disputed Legacy, 1846–1990* (Karachi: Oxford University Press, 1992). In a number of instances, however, Lamb has no evidence to offer. He simply assumes that particular events occurred. His entire analysis is ridden with palpable hostility toward the Indian position and seems designed to exculpate the Pakistani leadership of any responsibility. For example, even though Lamb concedes that the principal organizer of the invasion, former Pakistani Major General Akbar Khan, had met with Liaquat Ali Khan, the Pakistani prime minister, as well as with other political notables, he assumes that Mohammed Ali Jinnah, the governor-general of Pakistan, was completely unaware of this conclave (p. 125). Yet Lamb is unwilling to make similar allowances to the Indian side. In noting that Sheikh Mohammed Abdullah visited Nehru in New Delhi in mid-October 1947, Lamb assumes that they *must* have discussed the Instrument of Accession (p. 132).

Pakistan's subsequent invasion of the state can be gleaned from three sources.[27]

One of these sources was written by H. V. Hodson, a former British civil servant closely connected with the process of the transfer of power. In his authoritative account of the final days of the British raj, Hodson categorically states that there was a distinct lack of enthusiasm among the Indian cabinet about the accession of Kashmir. Hodson noted:

> From these records it is abundantly clear, first, that the advice the Maharajah received was not to hurry but to consider the will of his people in deciding which new Dominion to join; secondly, that not only the Viceroy but also Pandit Nehru and Sardar Patel openly accepted the possibility that Kashmir might accede to Pakistan; thirdly that the Viceroy went to great lengths to prevent even an appearance of undue political pressure on Kashmir from the Congress; and finally that Pandit Nehru's personal emotions were deeply engaged, though at this stage they were more concerned with the fate of Sheikh Abdullah and the rights of the people than with the accession of the State.[28]

Furthermore, Hodson provides circumstantial evidence of Pakistan's complicity in aiding and assisting the tribal invasion. He thus substantially corroborates the second source, the account written by former Pakistani Major General Akbar Khan. Specifically, Hodson mentions that Sir Frank Messervy, commander-in-chief of the Pakistan armed forces, cautioned Liaquat Ali Khan against assisting the tribal invasion in Poonch. Messervy issued this warning after Sir George Cunningham had called him to ascertain the Pakistani government's position on assistance to the rebels. Sir George had been prompted to ask this question because he had learned that Khan Abdul Qaiyum Khan, the chief minister

---

[27] Pakistan's role in aiding and abetting the tribal rebellion is well documented in Khan, *Raiders in Kashmir*. The best evidence on the legality of the accession can be found in Hodson, *The Great Divide*. A third source, which seeks to address forthrightly the Pakistani questions about the conditions under which the Instrument of Accession was signed, is Jha, *Kashmir, 1947*.

[28] Hodson, *The Great Divide*, 443.

of the North West Frontier Province, had been encouraging tribesmen to go to Kashmir in addition to making provision for trans-
portation. After warning Khan, Messervy left for London on military business. On his return to Rawalpindi, he sent one of his
officers on some pretext to the house of the commissioner of
Rawalpindi. To his surprise he discovered the commissioner pre-
siding over a meeting with a number of tribal leaders.[29]

In the third source, a prominent Indian journalist and political
commentator, Prem Shankar Jha, provides further corroboration
of Hodson's arguments and evidence. With evidence gathered in a
careful perusal of the records at the India Office Library in London, Jha demonstrates that there was substantial Pakistani complicity in planning and executing the invasion.

Hodson's account suggests that Pakistan may well have been
able to obtain Kashmir if it had not acted so precipitously. Given
Kashmir's Muslim-majority population and its physical proximity,
a plebiscite, like that in Junagadh, would have been virtually
inevitable.

From a purely *legal* sense, as specified under the terms of the
Indian Independence Act, Maharaja Hari Singh had the right to
join either India or Pakistan. The act had vested this right in the
hands of the rulers of the various princely states.

Kashmir's political evolution within the Indian Union was sui
generis: It was the only Muslim-majority state that acceded to the
Indian Union in 1947.[30] The reasons for its unique politics and for
the insurgency that broke out in 1989 need explanation, to which
I turn in the next chapter.

---

[29] Ibid., 447. Hodson's account provides only circumstantial evidence of
Pakistani complicity. It is nevertheless a far cry from Lamb's efforts to
suggest that the rebellion was entirely spontaneous and that the Pakistani
political leadership remained aloof from the proceedings.

[30] The terms of Kashmir's accession to the Indian Union form the legal basis
of the Indo-Pakistani dispute over Kashmir. For the most pro-Pakistani
account, see Lamb, *Kashmir: A Disputed Legacy.*

2

Political mobilization and
the onset of the insurgency

What factors explain the rise of violent ethnoreligious sentiment
in Kashmir in 1989? Scholars and other observers have proffered
a variety of answers to this question.[1] Most of the explanations
given so far have important shortcomings, however. At worst,
they are partisan and polemical. At best, they amount to only
partial explanations. Herein I hope to craft a more reasoned explanation that draws on a well-established body of literature in the
field of political science and that takes a more careful look at the
conditions under which the insurgency did (and did not) develop
in Kashmir.

EXPLAINING THE CRISIS

The various arguments that have been adduced to date can be
separated into four broad categories.

[1] See, for example, Shaheen Akhtar, *Uprising in Indian-Held Jammu and
Kashmir* (Islamabad: Institute of Regional Studies, 1991); Robert G. Wirs-
ing, *India, Pakistan, and the Kashmir Dispute: On Regional Conflict and
Its Resolution* (New York: St. Martin's, 1994); *Facets of a Proxy War* (New
Delhi: Government of India, 1993); Jagmohan, *My Frozen Turbulence in
Kashmir* (New Delhi: Allied, 1991); and Prem Shanker Jha, "Frustrated
Middle Class: Roots of Kashmir's Alienation," in *Secular Crown on Fire:
The Kashmir Problem,* ed. Asghar Ali Engineer (Delhi: Ajanta, 1991), 34–
7.

Variant one: Pakistan's not-so-hidden hand

Apologists for the government of India contend that the crisis is little more than a function of Pakistan's sponsorship of terrorism in Kashmir. They contend that Pakistan has engaged in a systematic strategy of infusing Islamic fundamentalist ideology into the Kashmir valley since the late 1970s. By providing large sums of money, Pakistan made possible the rapid growth in the number of *madrassas* (Islamic schools) throughout the valley. In these *madrassas*, pupils were steadily indoctrinated in the precepts of fundamentalist Islamic thought and encouraged to challenge the writ of the secular Indian state.

In addition to this process of inculcating fundamentalist Islamic notions, the government of Pakistan—and, more specifically, the Pakistani army's Inter-Service Intelligence (ISI) agency—actively recruited Kashmiri youth from the valley and lured them across the border to Pakistan, where they were trained in guerrilla warfare, were given weaponry, and were fashioned into an organized fighting force. Then these trained guerrillas imbued with Islamic fervor were infiltrated back into the valley beginning in the late 1980s. Once in the valley, they set about an extensive campaign of violence and terror. The collapse of the Soviet Union and the concomitant rise of fundamentalist Islamic sentiment, the argument goes, facilitated these activities. Visions of an Islamic confraternity extending from the Kashmir valley across Pakistan and Afghanistan and into Central Asia animated the guerrillas and their supporters within the valley.[2] This argument further holds that the insurgency would promptly dissipate if Pakistan ceased

---

[2] In July 1989, a prominent Indian defense publication, the *Indian Defence Review*, published a fictional account of "Operation Topac," a scheme that was designed to destabilize Indian Kashmir and was supposedly hatched in 1988 under the military dictatorship of General Mohammed Zia-ul-Haq of Pakistan. The article did not make clear that this was a fictional account, and the scenario soon gained popular currency in India. For an article that analyzes Pakistan's involvement in the Kashmir crisis and that relies partially on the scenario, see K. Subrahmanyam, "Kashmir," *Strategic Analysis*

inciting, arming, training, and providing sanctuary to the insurgents.

This argument is both incomplete and self-serving. It grossly exaggerates Pakistan's role in fomenting the insurgency. Pakistan's part in aiding the insurgency is incontrovertible; the insurgents have derived the bulk of their weaponry as well as much of their training from Pakistani sources. Their grievances against the Indian state, however, are not of Pakistan's making. Pakistan has simply exploited the existing discontent within a segment of Kashmir's population.

This argument also overlooks the significant role that the Indian state played in precipitating the crisis. The systematic corruption of the electoral process and the stifling of any honest opposition within an institutional context effectively pushed oppositional politics into the extraconstitutional arena.

Variant two: India's denial of self-determination

The government of Pakistan has offered its own explanation for the genesis of the crisis. A tract from a Pakistani government–sponsored organization has enumerated a number of factors that underlie the insurgency: "The current uprising in Kashmir is the outcome of multiple factors. These include historical betrayals, constitutional despotism, negation of socio-cultural identity, religious discrimination, economic deprivation and state repression, besides 43 years of misrule and manipulation by Delhi."[3] Each of these various factors, in turn, is adumbrated at some length.

The assertions made in the quotation above are far too sweeping. The government of India did little to negate the "socio-cultural identity" of the Kashmiris, Muslim or otherwise. Further-

---

23:11 (May 1990): 111–98. The government of India has also produced an unattributed pamphlet, *Pakistan's Targets: Punjab and Kashmir* (replete with gory photographs), which lists Pakistan's human and infrastructural targets in the two Indian states most affected by insurgencies, provides the names of prominent suspected terrorists, and lists the numbers of weapons captured from insurgents.
[3] Akhtar, *Uprising in Indian-Held Jammu and Kashmir,* 48.

more, within Kashmir there was little, if any, systematic religious discrimination. Finally, it is chimerical to suggest that Kashmir suffered from "economic deprivation"; for one example, in the Indian Union, Kashmir is the only state that guarantees free education through the undergraduate level. (The economic investment made by the central government in Kashmir will be expanded on later in this chapter.)

Two other important problems can be identified with this argument. First, it avoids any discussion of Pakistan's contribution to the maintenance of the insurgency. This help, as discussed above, has been substantial. Second, although all the factors that have been adduced are of some importance, neither the description nor the analysis suggests the relative weights that should be assigned to the particular factors in contributing to the ongoing crisis.

A markedly similar argument is propounded by Alistair Lamb, a British commentator on South Asian affairs. Lamb's detailed historical narrative is only seemingly impressive. From the very outset, he reveals his deep-seated belief in Indian malpractice. Evidence that is at best ambiguous is promptly marshaled to advance an argument baleful to the Indian position.[4] Mushtaqur Rahman offers a similar, though less sophisticated, version of Lamb's arguments.[5] Rahman's work, which is quite atheoretic, partisan, and derivative, offers no new insights.

Variant three: Ethnonational fervor

Social scientists have sought to provide more nuanced explanations for the birth of the insurgency. All their arguments are variations on a theme—namely, the emergence of ethnic subnationalism in Kashmir and its challenge to the Indian state. One such explanation, by Riyaz Punjabi, alludes to the breakdown of the ethos of Kashmiriyat, an ill-defined, almost ineffable concept of the

[4] Alistair Lamb, *Kashmir: A Disputed Legacy, 1846–1990* (Karachi: Oxford University Press, 1992).
[5] Mushtaqur Rahman, *Divided Kashmir: Old Problems for India, Pakistan, and the Kashmiri People* (Boulder: Lynne Reinner, 1996).

confluence of Islamic, Hindu, and uniquely Kashmiri cultural strains in the region.[6] This attempt to spell out the features of Kashmiriyat explains:

> The lineage of [the] Kashmiri people had given them distinctive looks; the fusion and assimilation of varied faiths and cultures had resulted in their particular and specific ethnicity. The land, the climate, the geography shaped the evolution of their particular ethnic profile. A common language bound them together into a distinct cultural grouping.[7]

In effect, this argument implies that religious identity constituted only one facet of Kashmiri ethnic identity. As to how this syncretistic identity unraveled, contributing to ethnic fratricide in the 1980s, Punjabi correctly, if less than persuasively, contends that the willingness of the central government to promote and sustain unpopular regimes in the valley steadily alienated the Muslim population. Consequently, he argues, the traditional bonds that had linked Hindus and Muslims in this shared vision of Kashmiriyat came apart. The Muslims of the valley no longer had much affinity for their Hindu counterparts or for the established Muslim leadership.

Punjabi's overall argument has more explanatory power than most other attempts. However, it does not account for the timing of the insurgency. He describes the insurgency as a consequence of a series of specific events. Furthermore, Punjabi's explanation fails to clarify two important issues: At what point did this composite Kashmiri identity start to fragment, and why did its disintegration necessarily contribute to a violent secessionist movement?

Ashutosh Varshney offers a more complex argument.[8] He con-

---

[6] Riyaz Punjabi, "Kashmir: The Bruised Identity," in *Perspectives on Kashmir: The Roots of Conflict in South Asia*, ed. Raju G. C. Thomas (Boulder: Westview, 1992), 131–52. For an alternative formulation of the concept of Kashmiriyat, see T. N. Madan, "Meaning of Kashmiriyat: Cultural Means and Political Ends," in *Kashmir: Need for Sub-continental Political Initiative*, ed. Gull M. Wani (New Delhi: Ashish Publishing House, 1995).

[7] Punjabi, "Kashmir: The Bruised Identity," p. 137.

[8] Ashutosh Varshney, "Three Compromised Nationalisms: Why Kashmir Has Been a Problem," in *Perspectives on Kashmir*, ed. Thomas, 191–234.

tends that the origins of the insurgency have to be sought in the competing claims of three variants of nationalism: religious, secular, and ethnic. All three versions of nationalism, Varshney contends, were compromised, in South Asia in general and Kashmir in particular, owing to the exigencies of nation-building and political expediency.

At one level, Varshney's argument is quite sophisticated and accurate. The Kashmir problem does involve a clash of national visions, however compromised. But this argument still fails to explain the specific timing of the insurgency. If the decline of secular nationalism is one of the factors behind the insurgency, then why did the insurgency not break out in the 1950s, after Sheikh Abdullah, the first prime minister of Jammu and Kashmir, was dismissed under pressure from Hindu nationalist organizations in Jammu for his putative disloyalty to the Indian Union?

Another drawback with Varshney's analysis is that he fails to effectively link the theoretical corpus with his historical narrative. His account depends more on other, extraneous factors—the intrusion of cold war politics into the region, for example. Furthermore, he locates the more immediate causes of the insurgency in the pull of Indian politics in the waning days of Prime Minister Indira Gandhi's regime.

Variant four: Circumstantial accounts

A final category of literature consists of historical and narrative accounts of the insurgency. These works are of varying quality, but none provides a theoretical explanation of the origins of the crisis. Ajit Bhattacharjea's book provides one of the best historical and analytic accounts of the political forces that contributed to the crisis.[9] A second journalistic account, by Tavleen Singh, fails to meet the standards set by Bhattacharjea. Her account, though rich in detail, has an informal tone and is largely anecdotal. She

[9] Ajit Bhattacharjea, *Kashmir: The Wounded Valley* (New Delhi: UBSPD, 1994).

emphasizes personalities and events at the cost of careful and dispassionate analysis.[10]

A former Indian army officer, Rajesh Kadian, has also written a historical account of the insurgency. Kadian's grasp of the historical detail, though largely derivative, is impressive. That said, his analysis of the forces that led to the insurgency is limited and familiar. He locates the sources of the insurgency in the malfeasances of the Farooq Abdullah government, the rise of Islamic fundamentalist sentiment, and Pakistani interference in the politics of the state.[11]

Finally, British political scientist Vernon Hewitt has written a historically grounded account of the Kashmir crisis. Hewitt's work not only traces the historical antecedents of the Kashmir problem, but also places the problem in the context of the evolution of India's politics since independence. Yet Hewitt's work, like the other historical accounts, fails to utilize the substantial body of social science literature that exists on ethnonationalism and ethnic conflict.[12]

AN ALTERNATIVE ARGUMENT

In contrast to the specific explanations of the Kashmiri insurgency that have just been discussed, this book argues that the insurgency in Kashmir is the result of a fundamental paradox of Indian democracy: Kashmir represents both the mobilizational success and, simultaneously, the institutional failure of Indian democracy.

Indian national policies and programs produced political mobilization on a historically unprecedented scale across India and in Kashmir particularly. Yet at the same time, successive national governments with varying degrees of commitment to democracy

---

[10] Tavleen Singh, *Kashmir: A Tragedy of Errors* (New Delhi: Viking, 1995).

[11] Rajesh Kadian, *The Kashmir Tangle: Issues and Options* (Boulder: Westview, 1993).

[12] Vernon Hewitt, *Reclaiming the Past? The Search for Political and Cultural Unity in Contemporary Jammu and Kashmir* (London: Portland Books, 1995).

did little to promote the strengthening of institutional politics in Jammu and Kashmir. And it is this dichotomy—the increase in political mobilization against a background of institutional decay—that best explains the origins of the secessionist insurgency in Kashmir.

POLITICAL MOBILIZATION AND INSTITUTIONAL DECAY

What exactly is political mobilization, and how does it take place? Political mobilization involves a form of political awakening and is reflected in citizens' desire for political participation. Politically mobilized groups seek to influence the political process directly in those areas in which it affects their everyday lives. The evidence of such mobilization and the resulting activism, of course, is a matter of degree. In certain political cultures, groups may be conscious of their political rights but nevertheless remain deferential and avoid challenging the existing order.[13] In other contexts, political mobilization can lead to increased political activism, which often produces agitational politics.[14]

What brings about political mobilization? Political mobilization results in part from increased literacy, media exposure, and economic development.[15] As groups acquire greater literacy and as their educational opportunities expand, they become increasingly aware of the sociopolitical forces that affect their lives. Furthermore, they become increasingly cognizant of the prospects for economic improvement. Accordingly, they begin to seek to influence the very forces that shape them. Thus in many democratic societies, political mobilization has produced increasing demands

---

[13] On this point, see Carole Pateman, "The Civic Culture: A Philosophic Critique," in *Political Culture Revisited,* ed. Gabriel A. Almond and Sidney Verba (Newbury Park: Sage Publications, 1989).

[14] See James Manor, "How and Why Liberal and Representative Politics Emerged in India," *Political Studies* 38:1 (March 1990): 20–38.

[15] See Samuel P. Huntington, *Political Order in Changing Societies* (New Haven: Yale University Press, 1968).

for the removal of institutional, cultural, and economic barriers to adult franchise.[16]

Political mobilization occurred early in India, and it defied the conventional pathways. Long before the advent of mass literacy, during the nationalist struggle for independence, large numbers of India's adult populace entered the political arena. Under the extraordinary political leadership of Mohandas Gandhi, the Indian National Congress was transformed from an upper-middle-class, Anglicized entity into a broad-based mass political party. Many of Gandhi's political strategies, such as the famous Salt March, successfully mobilized India's indigent peasantry. By leading mass campaigns of civil disobedience, Gandhi successfully inculcated notions of political accountability and franchise.

In independent India, several factors strengthened and expanded on Gandhi's legacy. India started its independent history with universal adult franchise—at least notionally. Subsequently, through the experience of elections at municipal, state, and national levels, increasing numbers of Indians became aware of the relationship between adult franchise and public policy. Growing educational opportunities and concomitant increases in literacy and media exposure fueled the momentum of political mobilization in India. One measure of the quickening pace was the steady increase in voter participation in both state and national elections.

Few if any postcolonial nations can claim the same breadth of political mobilization and institution-building as was found in India. The uniqueness of the Indian experience can be attributed

---

[16] One of the more important comparative discussions of the social transformations that engendered liberal democracy and the expansion of the franchise is Barrington Moore, *The Social Origins of Dictatorship and Democracy: Lord and Peasant in the Making of the Modern World* (Boston: Beacon, 1966). For an especially trenchant critique of the rhetoric employed in attempts to prevent social change and the expansion of civil and political rights, see Albert Hirschmann, *The Rhetoric of Reaction* (Cambridge, Mass.: Belknap Press of Harvard University, 1991).

in large measure to certain structural features of the Indian nationalist movement.[17] Specifically, the principal nationalist organization, the Congress Party, transformed itself into an organization that sought to represent the interests of all Indians. Furthermore, as Rajni Kothari pointed out in his seminal study of Indian politics, the Congress Party emerged in the postindependence era as a pluralist organization.[18] Internal debate within the party became a well-established norm; formulating the party's platform on crucial issues necessarily involved negotiation and compromise among various factions, ideological and regional. These well-embedded principles of negotiation and compromise provided the basis of democratic political development. Consequently, unlike other postcolonial regimes in the developing world, India was remarkably well equipped for the tasks of nation-building. In fact, in the first two decades of its independent history, it successfully contended with many of the "fissiparous tendencies" that had been forecast for its future.[19] For example, through the States Reorganization Act of 1956 and the development and implementation of the tri-language formula, India effectively dealt with the perils of linguistic agitation.[20]

There is little question that India's success with democratic institution-building and the tasks of national consolidation owes much to the structure of its nationalist movement. Yet the role of postcolonial political leadership cannot be overlooked. Prime Minister Jawaharlal Nehru, for one, played a critical role in nurturing democratic political institutions and practices. Among other things, Nehru recognized the vital importance of the federal system in India. A nation-state with every conceivable form of ethno-

---

[17] Judith Brown, *Modern India: The Origins of an Asian Democracy* (Oxford: Oxford University Press, 1994).

[18] Rajni Kothari, *Politics in India* (Boston: Little, Brown, 1972).

[19] Selig Harrison, *India: The Most Dangerous Decades* (Princeton: Princeton University Press, 1960).

[20] Jyotirindra Das Gupta, *Language Conflict and National Development: Group Politics and Language Policy in India* (Berkeley: University of California Press, 1970).

religious and ethnolinguistic cleavage simply cannot be governed through centralized dictates. His successors, most notably Indira Gandhi and Rajiv Gandhi, did little to perpetuate Nehru's practices and the institutions that he had striven to fashion and maintain, however.[21] In fact, faced with the extraordinary task of governing a polyethnic society, both Indira and, to a lesser extent, Rajiv Gandhi increasingly deinstitutionalized Indian politics. The imperatives of political survival drove Indira Gandhi and her son and successor steadily toward plebiscitary and personalized politics. Furthermore, they not only concentrated power in New Delhi but also increasingly resorted to coercive strategies to deal with any challenges to the national government's authority. Demands for autonomy were consistently misidentified as threats to the unity and integrity of the state. All too often, the characterization of these autonomist demands as threats to India's unity, along with the coercive strategies that were used to deal with the perceived threats, only magnified them. The Indian state responded with greater force, exacerbating the initial problem in a cycle of coercion.[22]

The process of deinstitutionalization that took place in India from the middle of the 1960s cannot be attributed solely to the personalities of and the policies adopted by Nehru's successors. Such an argument is facile and distorts the historical record. In addition to the personal proclivities of Mrs. Gandhi and her son and successor, Rajiv, there were longer-term structural factors that contributed to institutional decay in India. These included the shrinking electoral base of the Congress Party, the concomitant rise of new social groups in Indian politics, and the fragmentation of the electoral base along ethnoreligious, regional, and class lines. These factors, in turn, spawned the growth of a plethora of political parties, many of which came to the fore after the 1967 general

---

[21] Paul R. Brass, *The Politics of India since Independence,* 2d ed. (Cambridge: Cambridge University Press, 1994).

[22] For a discussion of the growth of and reliance on coercive state power in India, see Kuldeep Mathur, "The State and the Use of Coercive Power in India," *Asian Survey* 32:4 (April 1992): 337–49.

elections.[23] With the end of Congress dominance in much of India, other political parties forged political coalitions in several state assemblies. The Congress Party won a clear majority in the legislative assemblies of only seven states—Andhra Pradesh, Assam, Gujarat, Haryana, Madhya Pradesh, Maharashtra, and Mysore (now Karnataka). The Congress, distressed at its ouster from various state assemblies, sought to expand the discretionary powers of state governors. Expansion of such powers would provide governors with enough latitude to call on the leader of whichever party, in the governors' judgment, would be able to command a stable majority in the assembly. This expansion of powers, which raised constitutional questions, became a subject of political controversy and an important cause of instability.[24]

The new entrants into the political arena also undermined democratic norms and procedures. Some of these parties, particularly the two Communist parties, the pro-Soviet Communist Party of India (CPI) and the pro-Chinese Communist Party of India (Marxist) (CPI/M), openly contested democratic norms and parliamentary procedures. Sensing a weakening of central authority, the Communists sought to mobilize India's poor and less privileged, particularly in Kerala and West Bengal, states where the Communists had emerged as substantial political forces. In West Bengal, in addition to the emergence of a Communist-dominated United Front government, a neophyte Maoist guerrilla movement developed in the border district of Naxalbari. This organization—the Communist Party of India Marxist-Leninist, or CPI (M-L), popularly known as the Naxalites—received both ideological and material support from the People's Republic of China. The CPI (M-L), unlike the other two Communist parties, made no pretense of its contempt for democratic institutions. Until a Congress Party government ruthlessly suppressed CPI (M-L) activities after 1972, the Communists wreaked havoc throughout much of West Bengal,

---

[23] For a detailed analysis of these forces and trends in Indian politics, see Francine Frankel, *India's Political Economy, 1947–1977: The Gradual Revolution* (Princeton: Princeton University Press, 1978).

[24] For a discussion of the problems that ensued, see ibid., 362–5.

killing landowners, attacking police stations, and assassinating government officials.[25]

Other parties, such as the ultranationalist Jana Sangh, the predecessor to today's Bharatiya Janata Party, sought to mobilize along caste and religious issues. Such mobilization contributed significantly to widespread political instability and communal violence.

The decline of the Congress Party as a nationwide force and the entry of a plethora of new players in the political arena left much of India in a state of turmoil in the late 1960s. This upheaval profoundly undermined well-established legal and administrative procedures, led to declining parliamentary norms, and promoted increasingly populist politics.

The post-Nehru political generation's record with institution-building is far from exemplary. However, even the post-Nehru phase of Indian politics has seen some remarkable success: namely, the political mobilization of vast segments of India's electorate. Although universal adult franchise was nominally present in India from the beginning of independence, in practice nearly five decades of electoral participation in national, state, and local elections played a formidable role in furthering the mobilization of India's electorate. The remarkable increase in literacy and the notable growth of mass media have also served to expand demands for political participation.

The combination of institutional decay and political mobilization can contribute to political instability. This argument, first formulated by Samuel Huntington, is precisely applicable to India's political evolution. Huntington argued that the processes of economic modernization generate increasing demands for political participation by opening up new opportunities for physical, social, and economic mobility.[26] These pathways of mobility are not forged without cost, however. Socioeconomic mobility and personal mobility also undermine bonds of community. Furthermore,

[25] For a discussion of the Naxalite agitation and its consequences, see Marcus Franda, *Radical Politics in West Bengal* (Cambridge, Mass.: M.I.T. Press, 1971).

[26] For the classic statement on this subject, see Huntington, *Political Order.*

as Myron Weiner has demonstrated, accelerating mobility in the context of scarce resources in a polyethnic society can lead to political mobilization along ethnic lines and can result in interethnic tensions.[27] In the absence of robust political institutions that can manage, channel, and limit these ever-increasing demands, political instability will ensue. These twin forces—institutional decay and political mobilization—explain the rise of the ethnoreligious separatist movement in Kashmir.

POLITICAL MOBILIZATION IN JAMMU AND KASHMIR

The growth of political mobilization in Kashmir occurred at a slower pace than in the rest of India. The reasons lie in Kashmir's peculiar political history. As mentioned in the preceding chapter, in the closing days of the nationalist struggle in India, Kashmir was under the tutelage of Maharaja Hari Singh, not the most enlightened of princely rulers. Steady opposition to his reign had gathered force as independence and partition approached. The principal opposition was organized behind Sheikh Mohammed Abdullah, who had originally sought to mobilize Muslims in Jammu and Kashmir and to exact concessions from the maharaja. Accordingly, Abdullah's political party, which was founded in October 1932, was initially known as the All Jammu and Kashmir Muslim Conference. Subsequently, under the influence of Jawaharlal Nehru, Abdullah broadened his political base and renamed the party the Jammu and Kashmir National Conference (but not without considerable and vigorous debate). During World War II the party moved closer to the principal nationalist organization, the Indian National Congress, and distanced itself from the Muslim League, led by Mohammed Ali Jinnah.[28] (The Muslim League

---

[27] Myron Weiner, *Sons of the Soil: Migration and Ethnic Conflict in India* (Princeton: Princeton University Press, 1978).

[28] Prem Nath Bazaz, *The History of Struggle for Freedom in Kashmir* (Karachi: National Book Foundation, 1954), 179. Also see Jyoti Bhusan Das Gupta, *Jammu and Kashmir* (The Hague: Martinus Nijhoff, 1968), 62.

was the principal political party promoting Muslim separatism in British India and was instrumental in the creation of Pakistan. Its support base was made up of the landed gentry in the United Provinces of northern India.) Within Kashmir, the National Conference spearheaded efforts to bring about political and economic reform. The platform announced by the National Conference in September 1944 proposed a new constitution that would lead to representative government based on universal adult franchise and that would guarantee civil and political rights to all Kashmiris. The platform also called for extensive state intervention in the economic arena to bring about equity and social justice.[29] Another organization, the Muslim Conference, founded in 1934 and led by Ghulam Abbas, gravitated toward Jinnah and the Muslim League.

Little question exists that Abdullah's National Conference enjoyed widespread support within the state.[30] Yet Abdullah's strategy of political mobilization, although populist, was not democratic.[31] The organizational structure of the National Conference belied its socialist ideology.[32] As a political party, it was constructed largely around the personage of Abdullah and his close advisers. Decision making was concentrated in the hands of the sheikh. Little internal dissent was permitted. Abdullah's proclivity to tightly grasp the reins of power contributed to tensions between

[29] Das Gupta, *Jammu and Kashmir,* 66–7.

[30] The best analysis of the role of Abdullah in the National Conference can be found in Ian Copland, "The Abdullah Factor: Kashmiri Muslims and the Crisis of 1947," in *The Political Inheritance of Pakistan,* ed. D. A. Low (New York: St. Martin's, 1991).

[31] For a detailed, if self-serving, account of Abdullah's strategies of mobilization and his rise to power, see Bazaz, *Struggle for Freedom in Kashmir.* Bazaz, one of Sheikh Abdullah's mentors, broke away from the National Conference in 1940 after Abdullah allied himself with Jawaharlal Nehru and the Indian National Congress. Along with another prominent Kashmiri political activist, Kanhya Lal Kaul, Bazaz created the Kashmir Socialist Party in March 1942. That party, which had a narrow electoral base, did not amount to much.

[32] This phenomenon was hardly unique to the Indian political context. For the classic statement of this discrepancy between ideology and organization, see Robert Michels, *Political Parties: A Sociological Study of the Oligarchical Tendencies of Modern Democracy* (New York: Dover, 1959).

him and some of his most trusted lieutenants, principally Mohiud-din Karra, Maulana Masoodi, and Mirza Afzal Beg.

Abdullah's successors, with the possible exception of G. M. Sadiq, perpetuated the sheikh's authoritarian ways. As a result, no honest political opposition was ever allowed to develop in the state. As an early analyst of the politics of Jammu and Kashmir wrote:

> Time has now come to pass judgement on Abdullah's Government. Internally, it was hardly democratic. Opposition was suppressed, and civil liberties existed in name and for those who shared his views. His economic views were radical but he combined them with the workings of the like-minded totalitarian Governments elsewhere. He enjoyed tremendous popularity, yet resorted to questionable means to gain an electoral majority.[33]

Such policies significantly limited the growth and development of political institutions within Jammu and Kashmir. Consequently, even though a Constituent Assembly was convened in October 1951 and the state adopted its own constitution, the mechanisms of political representation were stunted from the outset. Unlike elections in the rest of India, Jammu and Kashmir elections were largely a farce. The National Conference and its operatives dominated the politics of the state.[34] Furthermore, the central government in New Delhi did little to stay the hand of the National Conference as long as it did not question the accession of Jammu and Kashmir into the Indian Union.

IMPROVING SOCIOECONOMIC CONDITIONS IN THE STATE

The political record of the National Conference was not limited to sheer skulduggery. The party did much, particularly in its initial

---

[33] Das Gupta, *Jammu and Kashmir*, 209.
[34] The one important exception was the communal Praja Parishad Party, led by Prem Nath Dogra and Balraj Madhok, which had a substantial following in the Hindu-dominated areas of Jammu. The Praja Parishad was formed in November 1947.

years in power, to improve socioeconomic conditions in the state. In so doing, it laid the foundation for the emergence of a new generation of Kashmiris—better educated than their predecessors, more conscious of their political rights and prerogatives, and impatient with the earlier generation of political leaders. This new generation would eventually come to challenge the writ of the National Conference.

Maharaja Hari Singh had done little to ameliorate the social and economic backwardness of his kingdom. During his reign, the principal source of income, land, was held largely by two classes of landlords: *jagirdars* and *muafidars*. The *jagirdars* owned entire villages from which they extracted revenue. The monarch had granted them these *jagirs,* some in perpetuity. The *muafidars* were individuals, such as pandits (Brahmins) or *faqirs* (Muslim mendicants), who paid no taxes on the lands assigned to them by the monarch. These two groups of landlords rented out most of the available cultivable land within the state under conditions resembling medieval exploitation.[35]

One of the first political initiatives that the National Conference undertook after winning office was to abolish landlordism. Two pieces of legislation were passed in 1950: the Abolition of Big Landed Estates Act and the Distressed Debtors Relief Act. The first confiscated all cultivable land greater than twenty-three acres and either distributed the land to landless peasantry or converted it into state property. The second directive created a board that instituted policies for the relief of debt. Although these initiatives alienated a significant segment of the Jammu-based Hindu landed gentry, they won Abdullah the powerful loyalty of lower- and middle-class Muslims and Hindus alike.[36] Long after Abdullah's dismissal by the prime minister and his incarceration in 1953, large segments of the Kashmiri peasantry remained loyal to him. And even though subsequent National Conference governments proved to be inept and corrupt, Abdullah's personal standing in Kashmir remained largely undiminished.

[35] Das Gupta, *Jammu and Kashmir,* 188.   [36] Ibid., 189–90.

TRACING THE PROCESS OF
POLITICAL MOBILIZATION

The socioeconomic transformation that was begun in Kashmir under Sheikh Abdullah was continued by his successors and, increasingly, by the national government in New Delhi. The electorate changed from a politically passive to an increasingly politically aware and assertive population.[37] One caveat needs to be made at the very outset of this section: It is virtually impossible to assert a definite causal link between the indicators of socioeconomic development and growing political consciousness. In many authoritarian states, despite phenomenal rates of economic growth, political awareness and demands for political participation have remained quite low.[38] The Indian case, as will be argued, is indeed exceptional. As they acquired more and more education, were exposed to mass media, and acquired a modicum of social and physical mobility, Kashmiris became aware that the free exercise of adult franchise existed in virtually all other parts of India. Only in the Kashmir valley were elections routinely compromised. This discrepancy, in large measure, caused the pangs of discontent. After years of frustrated attempts at meaningful political participation, and in the absence of institutional means of expressing dissent, resort to more violent methods became all but inevitable.

What, then, were the mechanisms of political mobilization in Kashmir? A vital one was the growth of educational institutions. Table 2.1 illustrates one measurement of increased access to education: the dramatic growth in literacy rates during the 1960s and 1970s. In the ten years from 1971 to 1981, the overall literacy rate

[37] For a sophisticated discussion of the economic transformation of Jammu and Kashmir, see M. L. Misri and M. S. Bhatt, *Poverty, Planning, and Economic Change in Jammu and Kashmir* (New Delhi: Vikas, 1994). Some economists would argue that the increasing flow of money from the central government into Jammu and Kashmir created a dependent economy in the state. (Author interview with senior Jammu and Kashmir government economist, New Delhi, January 1994.)

[38] See, for example, the discussion in Robert Wade, *Governing the Market* (Princeton: Princeton University Press, 1992).

Table 2.1. *Literacy rates in Jammu and Kashmir, 1961–81*

	Male	Female	Total population	Ten-year percentage increase
1961	16.97	4.26	11.03	
1971	26.75	9.28	18.58	68.45
1981	36.29	15.88	26.67	43.54

Source: Census of India, 1981: Handbook of Population Statistics (New Delhi: Government of India, 1988), 60.

in Jammu and Kashmir grew by more than 43 percent, the third-fastest growth rate in the nation.[39] Tables 2.2 and 2.3 show a similarly dramatic increase in enrollments in educational institutions.

In addition to the growth of formal education, Kashmir has seen a dramatic growth in *madrassa* education, particularly in the last ten to fifteen years.[40] The growth of *madrassas* (Islamic schools) received a tremendous boost after 1983, with the emigration of a significant number of Bangladeshi *maulvis* (Muslim religious teachers) from the eastern Indian state of Assam to Kashmir after the massacre of many inhabitants of the Assamese village of Nellie. The massacre was part of a rising anti-immigrant sentiment against Bangladeshi Muslims who had been migrating across the porous border from Bangladesh into Assam. Now these *maulvis* settled in Kashmir in the hope that they would be more secure in the nation's only Muslim-majority state.[41]

The growth in educational facilities at a variety of levels meant that increasing numbers of Kashmiris were becoming literate. Theoretically, literacy enables individuals to have a better comprehension of the social and political forces that affect their lives. Consequently, they gain an increased awareness of politics at local, national, and international levels.

[39] For the ranking of literacy growth rates, see Afsir Karim and the Indian Defence Review Team, *Kashmir: The Troubled Frontiers* (New Delhi: Lancer, 1994), 188, 250.

[40] Jagmohan, *My Frozen Turbulence in Kashmir,* 179–80.

[41] I am indebted to a senior Indian government official for this insight. (Author interview, New York City, July 1995.)

Table 2.2. *Educational enrollments in Jammu and Kashmir, 1950–93*

Year	Primary	Middle	Secondary	General colleges	Universities	Engineering colleges	Medical colleges	Agricultural colleges
1950–1	78,000	20,000	5,600	2,779	—	—	—	—
1960–1	216,000	60,000	22,000	8,005	174	171	182	—
1968–9	362,000	105,000	51,000	16,718	1,285	1,280	848	80
1980–1	537,800	167,200	83,600	15,828	3,351	1,286	1,072	294
1985–6	663,700	232,700	132,800	20,089	4,139	2,784	1,110	312
1992–3	940,000	370,000	262,000	34,000	NA	NA	NA	NA

Sources: Government of Jammu and Kashmir, Department of Planning and Development, Directorate of Economics and Statistics, *Digest of Statistics,* 1985–86 (Srinagar: Government Press, 1968); *Jammu and Kashmir: An Economic Profile* (New Delhi: Government of India, 1995), 18.

Table 2.3. *University enrollment levels in Jammu and Kashmir,*
1950–1 and 1976–7

		1950–1		1976–7	
		Number enrolled	% of population[a]	Number enrolled	% of (1981) population[a]
General	male	2,417		13,726	
	female	252		7,102	
Professional	male	50		2,986	
	female	10		545	
Special	male	109		370	
	female	5		80	
Total		2,843	.087%	24,809	.414%

[a] Population of Jammu and Kashmir in 1951 = 3,253,852; in 1981 = 5,987,389.
Sources: Government of Jammu and Kashmir, Department of Planning and Development, Directorate of Evaluation and Statistics, *Digest of Statistics, 1977–78,* vol. 2 (Srinagar: Government of Jammu and Kashmir, 1978), 271; Directorate of Census Operations, Jammu and Kashmir, *Census of India, 1981: A Portrait of a Population: Jammu and Kashmir* (Srinagar: Government of India, 1986), 11–12.

The expansion of mass media also bolstered the process of political mobilization. As shown in Table 2.4, between 1965 and 1984 tremendous growth occurred in the print media, in India in general and in Kashmir in particular. For example, in 1965, only 46 newspapers were published in Kashmir. Ten years later, 135 papers were being published. By 1991, the number had grown to 254. Essentially, in the span of approximately twenty-five years, the number of newspapers published grew by some 450 percent.[42]

In addition to the dramatic increase in the actual numbers of newspapers published, Kashmir also saw significant increases in newspaper circulation. Though some of the data is incomplete, it is nevertheless revealing. In 1982, total newspaper circulation in Kashmir was estimated to be around 119,000. Two years later,

[42] I am indebted to Professor Kanti Bajpai of the School of International Studies, Jawaharlal Nehru University, New Delhi, for these figures. They were compiled from *Mass Media in India* (New Delhi: Publications Division, Ministry of Information and Broadcasting, Government of India, various years). These volumes have been published more or less annually since 1978.

Table 2.4. *Number of newspapers published in Jammu and Kashmir and in India as a whole, 1965–84*

	1965	1970	1975	1984
Jammu and Kashmir	46	102	135	203
All India	7,906	11,306	12,423	21,784

Sources: Mass Media in India, 1978 (New Delhi: Publications Division, Ministry of Information and Broadcasting, Government of India, 1978); *Mass Media in India, 1986* (New Delhi: Publications Division, Ministry of Information and Broadcasting, Government of India, 1987).

the circulation had risen to 192,000. In another five years, the figure was 369,000. By 1990, newspaper circulation was down sharply—to only 280,000. In 1992 it stood at 297,000.[43] (This abrupt downturn in circulation may be due to militant threats against various newspapers, as well as to the flight of many Kashmiris from the valley.)

Finally, Kashmir, along with other parts of India, has seen a significant growth in the electronic media, especially television and video and audio tape recorders. Owing to its location, Kashmir was one of the earliest states in India to have access to television. (The Indian government wanted to ensure that the Kashmiris were not exposed only to Pakistani broadcasts.) The ability of even rural Kashmiris to receive television and radio broadcasts was facilitated by the tremendous state-driven process of rural electrification (Table 2.5). Thus in 1972 Srinagar was the third "television center" to be commissioned in India, after Delhi and Bombay. Access to television broadcasts, of course, depends on the availability of television sets. Making accurate estimates of the numbers of television sets in use is problematic, but the fact that licenses were supposed to be obtained before the purchase of a television set does provide some basis for an assessment. In 1981, for example, the Department of Posts and Telegraphs issued 3,262 licenses. By 1984, the last year that television licenses were issued, the

[43] Figures from *Mass Media in India,* various years.

Table 2.5. *Extent of rural electrification in Jammu and Kashmir, 1950–1 and 1976–7*

	Number of villages with a source of electrical power		
	Jammu	Kashmir	Ladakh
1950–1	3	12	0
1976–7	1,293	2,047	18

Source: Government of Jammu and Kashmir, Department of Planning and Development, Directorate of Evaluation and Statistics, *Digest of Statistics, 1977–78*, vol. 2 (Srinagar: Government of Jammu and Kashmir, 1978), 150.

number had increased to 20,896—a nearly sixfold increase. It should be noted that the number of licenses issued is, at best, an imperfect indicator; by the mid-1980s fewer and fewer individuals bothered purchasing television licenses. The most recent estimate, made in 1992, suggests that Kashmir had 118,000 television sets, or 1 per 65 residents.[44]

The availability of videocassette recorders (VCRs) and videotapes has greatly expanded the reach of television coverage. Statistics on the availability of VCRs in Kashmir are hard to come by. One can make some informed judgments, however, by examining the overall data for India. In 1982, it is estimated that the country had 180,000 VCRs, which accounted for 11.6 percent of those homes that had television sets. Only one year later, it was estimated that 530,000 VCRs were in existence—34.2 percent of television-owning homes. In 1984, the figure had risen to 610,000. Again, although no Kashmir-specific data is currently available, it is reasonable to surmise that Kashmir was not significantly different from other parts and states of India with regard to VCR and television ownership.

What inferences can be drawn from this admittedly suggestive data? It can be argued that given the dramatic expansion in literacy and media exposure, a generation of Kashmiris has now

[44] Ibid.

emerged that is far more conscious of its political rights and privileges. This generation is also most likely aware of political developments well beyond the valley of Kashmir and is far more politically sophisticated and knowledgeable than previous generations of Kashmiris—those who had been loyal to Sheikh Abdullah and his family.[45] The new, politically aware generation has proved unwilling to tolerate the skulduggery that has long characterized Kashmiri politics.

EXPLAINING POLITICAL DECAY

The literature of political development in the 1950s and 1960s assumed that, to use Robert Packenham's inimitable phrase, "all good things go together."[46] Namely, economic development would inevitably contribute to political development.[47] Political development, for the most part, was assumed to mean the development of democratic institutions.[48] Samuel Huntington in 1968 forthrightly questioned the premises of the first wave of the political development literature.[49] Far from contributing to democracy, Huntington argued, economic development may well lead to widespread political instability, especially in the absence of robust political institutions. Such institutions, he contended, were critical for maintaining political order in societies undergoing rapid economic modernization. Modernization, in Huntington's view, opened up new possibilities of social and economic mobility, reduced the familiar ties of kith

---

[45] Specifically, one event, the collapse of the Soviet Union in the late 1980s, profoundly animated a younger generation of Kashmiris. Many reasoned that if the might of the Soviet empire could be challenged, so could the writ of the Indian state.

[46] For an exposition and discussion of this thesis, see Robert Packenham, *Liberal America and the Third World* (Princeton: Princeton University Press, 1975).

[47] For an early critique of these premises of political development and nation-building, see Walker Connor, "Nation-Building or Nation-Destroying?" *World Politics* 24:3 (1972): 319–55.

[48] The literature on this subject is vast. Much of it was generated by funding provided by the Social Science Research Council (SSRC).

[49] Huntington, *Political Order*.

and community, and generated increasing demands for political participation. In the absence of well-developed political institutions that could mediate these demands, the quickening pace of economic modernization would give rise to political decay and eventually instability.[50] Of the vast majority of states in the postcolonial world, Huntington believed that India had considerable promise because of the strength of its political institutions: a highly professional civil service, a well-developed electoral system, and a political party (the Indian National Congress) that served as an umbrella organization for a variety of interests.

THE PATH TO INSTITUTIONAL DECAY

The decline of those promising political institutions in India, especially since the days of Indira Gandhi, has been commented on at length.[51] In Kashmir, the process of institutional decay started even before Mrs. Gandhi. The singular political tragedy of Kashmir's politics was the failure of the local and the national political leaderships to permit the development of an honest political opposition. From the time of independence to his dismissal from office in 1953, Sheikh Abdullah dominated the politics of Kashmir. Subsequent National Conference regimes used the prerogatives of office to prevent the growth of any meaningful opposition.

New Delhi's tolerance of such malfeasance seems a paradox. Kashmir, as India's only Muslim-majority state, was central to the nation-building enterprise in India.[52] Nehru and other national leaders contended that the existence of a Muslim-majority state in

[50] For a thoughtful critique of Huntington, focusing on his inordinate emphasis on "political order" and his inattention to questions of the legitimacy of institutions, see Mark Kesselman, "Order or Movement? The Literature of Political Development as Ideology," *World Politics* 26:1 (1973): 139–54.

[51] For an insightful discussion, see James Manor, "The Dynamics of Political Integration and Disintegration," in *The States of South Asia: Problems of National Integration,* ed. A. Jeyaratnam Wilson and Dennis Dalton (Honolulu: University of Hawaii Press, 1982).

[52] For an elaboration of this argument, see Šumit Ganguly, *The Origins of War in South Asia: The Indo-Pakistani Conflicts since 1947,* 2d ed. (Boulder: Westview, 1994).

India demonstrated that all faiths could thrive under the aegis of a secular state. Pakistan's irredentist claim on Kashmir, along with the state's ambiguous international status, made the Indian national leadership especially concerned about Kashmir's position within the Indian Union. As a consequence, the national political leadership, from Jawaharlal Nehru onward, adopted a singularly peculiar stand on the internal politics of Jammu and Kashmir: As long as the local political bosses avoided raising the secessionist bogey, the government in New Delhi overlooked the locals' political practices, corrupt or otherwise. As Prime Minister Nehru, with characteristic candor, wrote to the Kashmiri journalist and activist Prem Nath Bazaz in 1962: "It is true that political liberty does not exist there in the same measure as in the rest of India. At the same time there is much more of it than there used to be."[53]

As a result of local chicanery and national laissez-faire, every election except two (in 1977 and 1983) since the very first, in March 1957, was marked by corruption and deceit.[54] Over the years, any opposition to the National Conference was steadily driven out of the institutional arena.

ETHNORELIGIOUS MOBILIZATION

One final question needs to be answered: Why did the mobilization take place along ethnoreligious lines? Four factors are significant. First, the state is divided into districts that produce a religious division as well: Kashmir, Leh, Kargil, and Jammu. The valley of Kashmir is predominantly Muslim. The districts of Leh and Kargil (which until 1979 formed the single district of Ladakh) have mostly Buddhist and Muslim populations, respectively. Jammu, the fourth part of the state, is predominantly Hindu. The secular politics of the National Conference had little appeal among the Hindus of Jammu. Furthermore, acknowledging the difficulties of courting the Jammu

[53] Jawaharlal Nehru, as quoted in M. J. Akbar, *Kashmir: Behind the Vale* (New Delhi: Viking, 1991), 159.
[54] For a particularly harsh indictment of Abdullah's rule in Kashmir, see Prem Nath Bazaz, *Democracy through Intimidation and Terror* (New Delhi: Heritage, 1978).

Hindus, the National Conference had all but written off Jammu for electoral purposes.[55] Buddhist-dominated Leh was also outside the ambit of National Conference politics.

Second, the geographic isolation of the valley separated Kashmiri Islam from the larger currents of Muslim politics in India. Except on particular occasions, Muslims elsewhere in India rarely joined in common cause with their fellows in the valley.[56] In turn, the Muslims of the valley never developed extensive ties with Muslim communities in the rest of India. As a consequence, they did not air their grievances as part of the national community but as a regional subcommunity, with particular, parochial concerns. Furthermore, divisions existed even within the Muslim community of Kashmir. As Ian Copland has written:

> They were divided, first and foremost, by geography. Cut off from their co-religionists in Jammu by 15,000-foot mountain peaks, impassable in winter, the Muslims of Srinagar and its surrounding valley had evolved, over the centuries, a quite separate culture. While the people of Jammu spoke Dogri, a dialect akin to Punjabi, those of Srinagar spoke Kashmiri, which is closer to Persian; they built with brick and wood, rather than mud; and they dressed in a distinctive style typified, in the case of males, by the double pointed cap and the all-purpose cloak, the *farran*.[57]

Moreover, though it is difficult to demonstrate on the basis of systematic evidence, there is little question that Muslims face discrimination in the mainstream of Indian society. With no substantial Kashmiri Muslim expatriate community elsewhere in India, the Muslims of the valley were understandably reluctant to venture into the rest of the country to seek their fortunes.

Third, as has been observed in other contexts, notably in Iran and Egypt, when secular politics fails to offer adequate channels

---

[55] See Balraj Puri, *Simmering Volcano: Study of Jammu's Relations with Kashmir* (New Delhi: Sterling, 1983).

[56] One of those rare occasions resulted from the theft of the *moh-e-moqaddas* (a hair of the Prophet Mohammed) from the Hazratbal mosque in Srinagar in December 1963. News of this tragic incident set off rioting as far away as Calcutta.

[57] Copland, "The Abdullah Factor," 224.

for the expression of discontent, the only viable means that remains is the pursuit of political mobilization along ethnoreligious lines.[58] This pathway of protest had a long history in Kashmir. In the 1930s, Sheikh Abdullah's followers had battled those of Mirwaiz Yusuf Shah, a prominent Muslim religious and political leader. Furthermore, even after independence, a steady undercurrent of ethnoreligious sentiment had swirled around the Muslim fundamentalist Jammat-i-Islami Party. On occasion, Sheikh Abdullah had even encouraged the followers of the Jammat to instill a degree of fear in New Delhi. Abdullah's strategy was simple and effective: He threatened to unleash the forces of the Jammat unless New Delhi supported him unequivocally.[59]

A fourth and final factor contributed to the ethnoreligious direction of the movement: Pakistan, sensing an opportunity to weaken India's hold on Kashmir, funded, trained, and organized a loose, unstructured movement into a coherent, organized enterprise directed toward challenging the writ of the Indian state in Kashmir.[60] The Soviet withdrawal from Afghanistan in 1990 and the subsequent collapse of the Soviet Union greatly facilitated the task of arming and assisting the Kashmiri insurgents. Significant numbers of battle-hardened Afghan *mujahideen* could now be directed toward a new cause. These Afghans had more to offer than direct support; their experience of ousting the Soviets from

[58] For the Iranian case, see William O. Beeman, "Images of the Great Satan: Representations of the United States in the Iranian Revolution," in *Religion and Politics in Iran: Shi'ism from Quietism to Revolution,* ed. Nikki R. Keddie (New Haven: Yale University Press, 1983). For the Egyptian case, see Fouad Ajami, "The Sorrows of Egypt," *Foreign Affairs* 74:5 (September–October 1995): 72–88.

[59] Author interview with senior Indian government official, New York, July 1995.

[60] Allegations of Pakistan's involvement in Kashmir are legion in India. Apart from Indian allegations, dispassionate observers have provided ample evidence of Pakistan's complicity. See, for example, John Ward Anderson and Kamran Khan, "Pakistan Shelters Islamic Radicals," *Washington Post,* March 8, 1995, A21–A22; Edward W. Desmond, "Pakistan's Hidden Hand," *Time,* July 22, 1991, 23; and R. A. Davis, "Kashmir in the Balance," *International Defence Review* 4 (1991): 301–4.

Afghanistan provided a model of opposition and resistance to a powerful state and its well-organized military.

The success of the Palestinian *intifada* further reinforced both the violent and the Islamic fundamentalist aspects of the insurgent movement in Kashmir. Ironically, owing to the government of India's close links with the Palestine Liberation Organization, a sizable number of Palestinian students attended Kashmir University in Srinagar in the late 1970s and early 1980s. These Palestinian students became an important conduit for information about the success of the *intifada* against Israel. Their struggle against the Israeli armed forces in the occupied territories animated many university students in Kashmir.[61]

In transforming the socioeconomic landscape of Kashmir and producing a generation of politically aware Kashmiris while also allowing the political institutions in Kashmir to be stunted and corroded, the national- and state-level governments left open few institutional channels for the expression of political discontent and dissent. Demands for political autonomy were inappropriately construed as incipient moves toward secession. Inevitably, this contradictory set of policies drove emerging generations of Kashmiris toward more extreme forms of political expression. Furthermore, as secular and institutional pathways of expressing political dissent were curbed, political mobilization and activism increasingly proceeded along an ethnoreligious dimension.

The next several chapters will juxtapose the political malfeasances of the Indian state with the simultaneous growth of political consciousness. Each chapter will examine these developments from a particularly salient period in the history of the state. These case studies will show that previous Pakistani efforts to foment a rebellion in Kashmir failed because of the political quiescence of an earlier generation of Kashmiris. And the final study, that of the most recent decade of Kashmir's history, will reveal the more proximate causes of the insurgency.

[61] Author interview with Mirwaiz Omar Farooq, Kashmiri Muslim religious leader and chairman of the All-Party Hurriyat Conference of Kashmir, New York, October 1995.

3

The past as contrast; or,
The dog that didn't bark

As discussed in the first chapter, two diametrically opposed arguments about the origins of the insurgency in Kashmir have acquired popular currency. The first, propagated by apologists for the government of India, suggests that the roots of the insurgency can be traced to Pakistan's instigation, indoctrination, and ultimately support for the secessionists. The second, espoused by the government of Pakistan and its sympathizers, holds that the secessionist movement represents the popular longing for self-determination of a primordial captive Kashmiri nation. As pointed out earlier, both arguments, though containing kernels of truth, are at best partial explanations. Looking at a specific era in Kashmir's recent history enables one to establish both statements as incomplete.

The period studied in this chapter extends from about 1962 to 1965. Both the adduced causes of the present insurgency were present during this era; yet, despite these conditions, an insurgency failed to materialize at this time. The government of India, since the ouster and subsequent incarceration of Sheikh Abdullah in August 1953, had turned a blind eye to the repressive regime of Kashmiri Prime Minister Bakshi Ghulam Mohammed. According to the most reliable accounts, the Bakshi regime had shown scant regard for tolerating honest dissent, had squelched civil liberties, and had engaged in widespread electoral malpractice.[1] Additionally, by 1963 the central government in New Delhi had started to integrate Jammu and Kashmir steadily into India, thereby eroding its special constitutional dispensation. Furthermore, the Pakistani leadership, having convinced itself that widespread disaffection existed in Kashmir, sought to foment a rebellion. Nevertheless, no popular uprising ensued. Consequently, neither offered explanation is entirely valid.

THE AFTERMATH OF
THE SINO-INDIAN BORDER CONFLICT OF 1962

In October 1962 India suffered the most humiliating military debacle in its postindependence history, at the hands of the Chinese People's Liberation Army (PLA).[2] The outcome of this conflict had far-reaching consequences for Indian foreign and defense policies. The harsh defeat that the Chinese PLA had inflicted on the Indian Army called into question some of the most deeply held precepts of Nehru's foreign and defense policies. Domestically, India's right-wing politicians, never at ease with either nonalignment or the low levels of military expenditures, now clamored for abandoning the former and dramatically increasing the latter. Internationally, Western conservatives felt that Nehru's moralizing posture now stood exposed. Nevertheless, Nehru refused to abandon nonalignment. But he was forced to concede ground on the question of increasing defense expenditures. Accordingly, a plan was drafted for the modernization of the armed services, principally the army and the air force. This scheme called for the creation of a forty-five–squadron air force equipped with modern jet aircraft, an expansion of the army to twenty-five divisions, including ten mountain divisions, and the improvement of border roads and airfields.

Pakistan, seeking to avoid American displeasure, chose not to

[1] See, for example, Jyoti Bhusan Das Gupta, *Jammu and Kashmir* (The Hague: Martinus Nijhoff, 1968). Also see Karan Singh, *Autobiography* (Delhi: Oxford University Press, 1994), and Mir Qasim, *My Life and Times* (New Delhi: Allied, 1992).

[2] The best account of this military debacle can be found in Steven Hoffman, *India and the China Crisis* (Berkeley: University of California Press, 1991).

open a second front during the Sino-Indian border war. Its restraint during the war was not lost on its Western allies. In the aftermath of the conflict, in December 1962, an Anglo-American mission led by Averell Harriman, a former U.S. ambassador to the Soviet Union, and Duncan Sandys, the British minister of defense, arrived in India.[3] The purpose of this mission was to persuade Nehru to settle the Kashmir dispute with Pakistan on terms that would be acceptable to Pakistan. Anglo-American leverage over India at this time was probably at its zenith. Nehru's own political standing, nothing short of primus inter pares previously, now seemed less than towering. Most important, India was actively seeking military assistance from the Western powers to contend with the Chinese military threat.[4]

BILATERAL NEGOTIATIONS

Despite considerable reservations, Nehru agreed to hold talks with Pakistan on Kashmir.[5] Shaken by the military debacle and depen-

[3] The background to this visit is worth recounting. The U.S. team, led by Averell Harriman, included James Grant, the deputy assistant secretary of state for Near East and South Asia; Roger Hilsman, then director of the Bureau of Intelligence and Research in the State Department; Paul Nitze, the assistant secretary of defense for international affairs; General Paul Adams, commander of Strike Command; and Carl Kaysen, of the National Security Council Staff. The group went to both New Delhi and Islamabad. At this time, the United States attached considerable significance to its military bases in Pakistan, which were critical for eavesdropping on the Soviet missile program. Consequently, there was great unwillingness within the Pentagon to lean on Pakistan for fear of the loss of the U.S. bases. Simultaneously, there was deep distrust of India within the Pentagon. Although both John Kenneth Galbraith and his successor, Chester Bowles, disagreed, Pentagon officials believed that India was untrustworthy because of its incipient relationship with the Soviet Union. (Author interview with the former assistant secretary of state for Near East and South Asia, Phillips Talbot, New York City, March 5, 1996.) See also Dennis Kux, *India and the United States: Estranged Democracies* (Washington, D.C.: National Defense University Press, 1993), 181–225.

[4] Kux, *Estranged Democracies*.

[5] Y. D. Gundevia, *Outside the Archives* (Hyderabad: Sangam, 1984), 249–52.

dent on the goodwill of the Western powers, he was hardly in a position to act otherwise. The talks opened in Rawalpindi on December 27, 1962. Zulfiquar Ali Bhutto represented Pakistan and Sardar Swaran Singh, India. The first round was ill-fated. Just as the talks were about to begin, Pakistan announced a border agreement with the People's Republic of China (PRC). Under the terms of this agreement, Pakistan ceded 2,050 square miles of territory in the northwestern portions of the state of Jammu and Kashmir to the PRC. Quite astutely, the wording clearly stated that the agreement did not prejudice a final settlement of the Kashmir dispute between India and Pakistan.[6]

On hearing of this agreement on Pakistani radio, the Indian delegation almost called off the talks. They eventually decided to continue with the talks, however, while New Delhi registered strong diplomatic protests to Pakistan and the PRC. The first round concluded with both sides restating their familiar positions on the dispute in general and the question of a plebiscite in particular: Pakistan insisted that a plebiscite had to be held to ascertain the wishes of the Kashmiris, and India insisted that, before a plebiscite would be held, Pakistan had to vacate the portion of Kashmir that it had seized in 1947–8. One small agreement was reached, however: Both sides agreed to desist from engaging in "adverse propaganda."[7]

The second round of talks was held in New Delhi from January 16 to January 19, 1963. This round inched forward after the usual litany of stating the respective formal positions. Sardar Swaran Singh proposed the partitioning of Kashmir, the disengagement of military forces, and the adoption of a "no war" declaration. By the third day the two sides agreed to seek "a possible overall, political settlement on a realistic basis, leading to the delimitation of an international boundary between India and Pakistan in Kashmir."[8] The Pakistanis did insist on an important caveat, however: The wishes of the Kashmiris would have to be taken into account in reaching any settlement.

[6] Das Gupta, *Jammu and Kashmir,* 298–300.
[7] Gundevia, *Outside the Archives,* 266.   [8] Ibid., 273.

The third round was held in Karachi February 8–10, 1963. During this round the negotiators held substantive discussions about the delineation of a border in Kashmir. Bhutto, now Pakistan's foreign minister, expanded the territorial demands to include the Kashmir and Chenab valleys as well as portions of Jammu. Unsurprisingly, this session accomplished little.[9]

The fourth session was held in Calcutta between March 12 and March 14, 1963. Again, the shadow of Sino-Pakistani collaboration loomed large over this meeting. On March 2, the Sino-Pakistani border accord had been formalized. Indian protests were prompt and vigorous. Specifically, Indian diplomatic spokesmen contended that this agreement violated the UN resolutions of 1948 and 1949, which enjoined both parties from unilaterally altering the status quo in Kashmir. Rejecting that charge, Pakistan's spokesmen accused India of the same. They contended that India's transformation of the constitutional arrangements in Kashmir amounted to an alteration of the status quo.

Just before the next round of talks, scheduled to be held in Karachi, G. Parthasarathi, the Indian high commissioner to Pakistan, returned to New Delhi. Parthasarathi had been given an Anglo-American proposal for the possible settlement of the Kashmir dispute. The crux of the proposal asked India to give up substantial portions of the Kashmir valley to Pakistan. In addition to this territorial concession, India was asked to make arrangements for increased "self-rule" for the inhabitants of the remaining portion of Kashmir. On learning of this proposal, Jawaharlal Nehru considered calling off the Karachi talks.[10]

After considerable deliberation, however, the Indians decided to attend the next round. The talks opened on April 21 and lasted until April 25. The Pakistanis pushed the Anglo-American proposal. The Indian side refused to budge, insisting that such a concession would not only undermine the Indus Waters Treaty of 1960 but also leave Ladakh indefensible. Curiously, despite this

[9] *Foreign Relations of the United States, 1961–63*, vol. 19 (Washington, D.C.: Government Printing Office, 1996), 495.
[10] Ibid., 290.

deadlock, Bhutto asked Sardar Swaran Singh for another meeting. This meeting started on May 14 and concluded on May 16. At this final round, Bhutto suggested two possibilities: either the valley be given to Pakistan after a specified period of time, or it be "internationalized" for a limited duration and then an attempt be made to "ascertain the wishes of the people."[11] In response, the Indian side refused to move beyond its initial proposals of altering the Cease-Fire Line (CFL). The two sides also held some desultory discussions about changing the troop deployments along the CFL. Eventually, with neither side showing much flexibility, the talks collapsed.

TROUBLES IN THE VALE

India's willingness to make significant territorial concessions to Pakistan had probably dissipated long before these protracted and ultimately unsuccessful negotiations. Indeed, in 1947 Nehru had publicly and unequivocally committed India to hold a plebiscite to ascertain Kashmir's future in the Indian Union. However, an American decision to supply arms to Pakistan in 1954 led to a hardening of his position. Domestic public opinion had become so inflamed that it would be exceedingly difficult, if not downright impossible, for him to carry through his earlier promise.[12]

No doubt with an eye toward cementing Jammu and Kashmir's relationship with the Indian Union, India started to dismantle the special provisions of Jammu and Kashmir. The chief minister of Jammu and Kashmir (still referred to as the prime minister) at this time was Bakshi Ghulam Mohammed. Though Bakshi did not belong to the Congress Party, he resigned at the behest of Prime Minister Nehru as part of a nationwide Congress Party initiative,

---

[11] Reached under the auspices of the World Bank, the Indus Waters Treaty is an agreement between India and Pakistan over the sharing and control of river waters in the two Punjabs.

[12] Personal communication with Escott Reid, former Canadian high commissioner to India, January 1991. Also see Escott Reid, *Envoy to Nehru* (New Delhi: Oxford University Press, 1981).

known as the Kamaraj Plan. Under this plan the Congress chief ministers in various states throughout India were asked to hand in their resignations to bring about a reorganization of the Congress Party.[13]

Just before stepping down from his position as prime minister, Bakshi said that in the future the prime minister of Jammu and Kashmir would be known as the chief minister. This change in nomenclature was significant. From now on, Jammu and Kashmir's principal elected position would be on a par with the chief ministers of other states in India. Kwaja Shamsuddin, a close associate of Bakshi's, succeeded him as prime (soon to be chief) minister.

THE HAZRATBAL EPISODE

Later that year, a troubling incident roiled the politics of the state. The Hazratbal mosque in Srinagar is the repository of the *moh-e-moqaddas* (a hair of the Prophet Mohammed). On December 26, 1963, the holy relic suddenly disappeared. The apparent theft of the relic led to disturbances throughout the valley as rumors about the perpetrators of this act became rife.[14] Indian Intelligence Bureau (IB) agents apparently recovered the relic and returned it to the mosque on January 3, 1964. Meanwhile, Maulana Mohammed Syed Masoodi, the former general secretary of the National Conference, had created an Action Committee for the recovery of the relic. Masoodi, an opponent of Bakshi's, insisted that the authenticity of the holy relic had to be verified by a panel of devout Muslims before his agitation would cease. The government in New Delhi decided that the situation in Kashmir was disturbed enough to merit attention. Accordingly, a senior Congress Party minister, Lal Bahadur Shastri, was sent to Srinagar. Shastri over-

---

[13] Paul R. Brass, *The Politics of India since Independence*, 2d ed. (Cambridge: Cambridge University Press, 1994), 37–38.

[14] For a detailed but self-serving account of the disappearance of the holy relic and its subsequent recovery, see B. N. Mullik, *My Years with Nehru: Kashmir* (New Delhi: Allied, 1971).

ruled the advice of the local officials who were opposed to the verification process and insisted that the verification take place. On February 3 clerics who controlled the shrine examined the relic and pronounced it authentic.[15]

In the wake of the Hazratbal crisis and with a view toward introducing more honest and efficient governance, Shastri prevailed on Shamsuddin to resign. On February 28 a new regime, with G. M. Sadiq, a leftist National Conference leader, as chief minister, assumed office. Maulana Masoodi, the Action Committee leader, now found a new cause to champion. On March 20 he publicly endorsed his organization's call for a plebiscite to determine the future of Kashmir. In an attempt to stave off further agitation, Sadiq came up with a novel strategy. He decided to release Sheikh Mohammed Abdullah, who had been languishing in prison since his arrest in August 1953. On April 8, after a Special Court withdrew all charges against the sheikh and his lieutenant Mirza Afzal Beg, both were unconditionally released.[16] Masoodi, despite his endorsement of a plebiscite, promptly rallied behind the enormously popular "lion of Kashmir," Sheikh Mohammed Abdullah. The president of the Action Committee, Mirwaiz Mohammed Farooq, whose uncle Mirwaiz Yusuf Shah had clashed with Sheikh Abdullah and his supporters in the 1930s, remained opposed to Abdullah and staunchly pro-Pakistani. Not surprisingly, a schism developed within the Action Committee between Abdullah's supporters and those of Mohammed Farooq. In June 1964 this rift became manifest with Abdullah deriding the Action Committee as a mere forum and not a political party. The Farooq loyalists broke away from the Action Committee and formed a group of their own, the Awami Action Committee. Abdullah, in turn, gave his allegiance to the Plebiscite Front of his lieutenant, Mirza Afzal Beg.[17] When not engaged in internecine conflict, these three groups sought to oppose the regime of G. M. Sadiq.

[15] Das Gupta, *Jammu and Kashmir*, 309.   [16] Ibid., 311.
[17] For an excellent description and analysis of the maneuvers of the various parties, see ibid., 320–22.

INTEGRATION INTO INDIA

The Sadiq regime, in the meantime, was in favor of integrating Jammu and Kashmir into the Indian Union. With Sadiq's critical co-operation, a number of provisions of the Indian Constitution were extended to Jammu and Kashmir. Specifically, on December 21, 1964, the president of India, Dr. Sarvapalli Radhakrishnan, issued an ordinance on two constitutional provisions that allowed President's Rule to be extended to the state. While President's Rule was in force, Parliament was empowered to make laws for the state. The extension of these provisions to the state was of no minor significance. Their passage meant that the government of Jammu and Kashmir could now be treated more or less like that in any other part of India. Through executive fiat, the special status that Kashmir had hitherto enjoyed was being denuded.

Other steps followed in quick succession. On March 30, 1965, the Kashmir Legislative Assembly passed the Constitution (Amendment) Bill, which brought about more significant changes. The title of the *sadr-i-riyasat* (head of state) was changed to "governor of Kashmir." Furthermore, the position would now be appointed by the president of India and not by the Kashmir Legislative Assembly. Finally, the announcement that the prime minister of the state would now be known as the chief minister, as elsewhere in India, was formalized.

Sheikh Abdullah protested these changes. His public speeches became increasingly intemperate and, on occasion, even took on a communal tenor.[18] Subsequently, Abdullah departed on a foreign tour that included stops in England, Egypt, Algeria, and Saudi Arabia. While on this tour, he repeatedly called for the right of "self-determination" for the Kashmiris. These persistent demands alone would have created problems for him with the government of India. But his decision to meet with Chou En-lai, the Chinese prime minister, while in Algiers and to seek assistance for "self-

---

[18] Ibid., 333.

determination" was more than any regime in India was prepared to countenance. On his return to New Delhi on May 8, 1965, Abdullah was arrested under the Defence of India Rules and whisked off to the southern Indian hill resort of Ootacamund.

Unlike his initial arrest in 1953, Abdullah's second arrest did not generate widespread popular disaffection in the Kashmir valley, for two reasons. First, the vast majority of the leaders of the Plebiscite Front, the most likely organizers of popular protest, were already incarcerated. Second, the Sadiq regime, anticipating protest, had taken some precautions. These two factors notwithstanding, the absence of popular protest was significant. Clearly, despite the disturbances in the wake of the Hazratbal episode, there was no great reservoir of popular discontent brimming in the valley. Abdullah's attempts to generate widespread dissatisfaction with the Sadiq government's decision to proceed in greater integration with India had failed to materialize.

The Pakistani leadership nonetheless perceived otherwise. As President Ayub Khan stated in a radio broadcast to the nation in early 1964:

> This upheaval was set in motion by the mysterious theft of the holy relic from the Hazratbal shrine, which injured the religious susceptibilities not only of the Muslims of occupied Kashmir but also of Pakistan. Subsequent events have, however, shown that the agitation was due also to the resentment of the people of Jammu and Kashmir at the subjugation by India and the Indian design to integrate their state.[19]

Contrary to Pakistani professions, however, the vast majority of Kashmiri Muslims did not perceive themselves as the members of a captive nation trapped in India's stranglehold.[20] This was to become amply apparent when Pakistan launched a carefully orchestrated attempt to stir a rebellion in the valley in the late

---

[19] Mohammed Ayub Khan, *Pakistan Perspectives* (Washington, D.C.: Embassy of Pakistan, n.d.), 47.

[20] For a discussion of various Pakistani statements about the plight of the Kashmiris, see Alistair Lamb, *Kashmir: A Disputed Legacy, 1846–1990* (Karachi: Oxford University Press, 1992).

summer of 1965. Kashmiris, far from rallying behind the Pakistani efforts, demonstrated their loyalty to the Indian state.

SLOUCHING TOWARD WAR

The Pakistani leadership of President Ayub Khan became quickly convinced of its own rhetoric about the plight of the captive Kashmiri nation. The foreign minister, Zulfiquar Ali Bhutto, was instrumental in promoting and reinforcing this belief. Bhutto's convictions, in turn, stemmed from several sources. First, in the wake of Nehru's death, he assumed that the potential for disintegration in India was great. As he wrote:

> The death of Jawaharlal Nehru has been a blow to India in more senses than one. It has released in that country centrifugal forces on an unprecedented scale. How long will the memory of dead Nehru inspire his countrymen to keep alive a polyglot India, the vast land of mysterious contradictions, darned together by the finest threads? . . . Nehru's magic touch is gone. His spellbinding influence over the masses has disappeared. The key to India's unity and greatness has not been handed over to any individual. It has been burnt away with Nehru's dead body.[21]

Second, on the basis of the popular discontent in the aftermath of the Hazratbal episode, he believed that widespread pro-Pakistani sentiment existed in the valley. These two flawed inferences in turn were reinforced by a third, bizarre, and essentially racist notion of the inherent martial prowess of the Pakistani (Muslim) army.[22]

In addition to these beliefs, Ayub, Bhutto, and much of the upper echelons of the Pakistani military were convinced that the Indian military rearmament program that had been started after

---

[21] Zulfiquar Ali Bhutto, as quoted in Dilip Mukherjee, *Zulfiquar Ali Bhutto* (Delhi: Vikas, 1972), 46–7.

[22] For an extended description and analysis of Pakistani beliefs and motivations that contributed to Pakistan's attempt to foment rebellion in Kashmir and the Indo-Pakistani war of 1965, see Šumit Ganguly, "Deterrence Failure Revisited: The Indo-Pakistani War of 1965," *Journal of Strategic Studies* 13:4 (December 1990): 77–93.

the Chinese military debacle of 1962 would, in the foreseeable future, narrow the military balance in India's favor.[23] As Air Marshal Asghar Khan, the chief of the Pakistani air staff, wrote:

> The build-up of the Indian Armed Forces had been causing great concern to all thinking people in the Pakistan Armed Forces. Under the guise of preparations against China they succeeded in securing substantial military aid from the United States and were building up a million-strong army, almost doubling their Air Force, increasing their naval strength and further enhancing their aircraft and tank production capacities. . . . Pakistan was faced with a very dangerous situation. If we did not face up to it and prepare ourselves immediately, the time would come when, having built up her Armed Forces sufficiently, India would be in a position to achieve her political objectives without recourse to war.[24]

Consequently, in Pakistani perceptions, "the window of opportunity" to seize Kashmir through the use of force was rapidly closing.[25]

The Pakistani politico-military elite found much support for their beliefs when they undertook a "limited probe" in the trackless wastes of the Rann of Kutch in the Indian state of Gujarat.[26] The purpose of this action was to clarify India's defense preparedness and commitments. Pakistan claimed some thirty-five hundred square miles of the Kutch, asserting that this area had been under the control of the Sind government before the partition of British India. In drawing up the boundaries of India and Pakistan in the western sector during the time of partition, the Radcliffe Commission had failed to make a ruling on the Rann of Kutch.

On April 9, 1965, Pakistani Rangers attacked an Indian military post at Sardar in Gujarat. The Indian army retaliated on April 10,

---

[23] For a discussion of India's rearmament plans after the 1962 Sino-Indian border war, see Lorne J. Kavic, *India's Quest for Security* (Berkeley: University of California Press, 1967).

[24] Asghar Khan, *The First Round* (Ghaziabad: Vikas, 1979), 7–8.

[25] For a revealing account of Pakistani military perceptions, see General Mohammed Musa, *My Version: India-Pakistan War, 1965* (Lahore: Wajidalis, 1983).

[26] The concept of a "limited probe" is discussed in Alexander George and Richard Smoke, *Deterrence in American Foreign Policy* (New York: Columbia University Press, 1974).

dislodging the Pakistanis. Border skirmishes continued for the next two months. Yet for at least three compelling reasons, the Indian side chose not to escalate the conflict. First, the Kutch did not represent significant or valuable real estate. Second, using mechanized armor was difficult because of the unsuitability of the terrain. Third, Indian supply lines were long and difficult, whereas the Pakistanis had comparatively favorable communications.[27]

In June, British mediation at the Commonwealth Prime Ministers' Conference proved successful, and a cease-fire was declared on June 30. Under the terms of this accord both parties agreed to return to the status quo ante. Subsequently, they agreed to refer the dispute to the International Court of Justice at the Hague for adjudication.

THE FAILURE OF "OPERATION GIBRALTAR"

The Pakistani leadership made a fundamentally flawed inference from the seemingly hesitant Indian military response: It assumed that the Indians lacked stomach for battle. This incorrect supposition strengthened their earlier resolve to foment a rebellion in Kashmir and then to seize the valley in a short, sharp attack. This plan, known as "Operation Gibraltar," was the brainchild of General Akthar Husain Malik, commander of the Pakistani army's Twelfth Division. The first phase of this plan involved infiltrating into the valley about five thousand lightly armed men, who would then instigate a mass uprising against Indian rule. In the second phase, taking advantage of the disturbed conditions in the valley, the Pakistani army would then move to seize Kashmir in a series of quick, decisive thrusts. The seizure of the valley would present the international community with a fait accompli.

The men for this guerrilla campaign were organized in the hill resort town of Murree on May 26, 1965. The group was composed of eight to ten "forces," each comprising six units of five companies. (Approximately 110 men were assigned to each company.) Each company was composed of regular troops of the so-

---

[27] Russell Brines, *The Indo-Pakistani Conflict* (London: Pall Mall, 1968), 288.

called Azad Kashmir Army, which was part of the Pakistani Army, and of *mujahid* and *razakar* irregulars.[28]

The infiltration started around August 5, 1965, along the 470-mile CFL in Jammu and Kashmir. Dressed as local inhabitants, the men carried mostly small arms, grenades, plastic charges, and radio equipment. Local inhabitants quickly discovered the infiltrators and turned them in to the authorities. The cooperation of the local populace with the infiltrators, assistance on which this operation was predicated, simply failed to materialize.[29] As a consequence, the rebellion that the Pakistanis had hoped to produce proved to be stillborn. Indian civilian and military organizations, alerted to the Pakistani plan, quickly moved to seal the routes of infiltration and vigorously hunted down those forces that had already entered the valley.

On August 14 a substantial infiltration took place into Jammu from the "Azad Kashmir" town of Bhimbar. Indian sources claimed that this infiltration marked the first involvement of Pakistani regular troops. Further, they asserted that the force supporting the infiltrators amounted to a battalion in strength. The Indian forces retaliated on August 15, crossing the CFL into Kargil. Here the Indian army occupied three mountain positions. The border skirmishes continued through the month of August. On September 1 the Pakistanis launched a major attack in the Bhimbar-Chhamb area. This attack, which signaled the beginning of the 1965 war, was code-named "Operation Grand Slam."[30]

CONCLUSIONS

The years between 1962 and 1965 saw the beginnings of the wearing away of the special status of Jammu and Kashmir as a

[28] The *mujahideen* were lightly trained civilian reserves. The *razakars* were a paramilitary force under army control. See ibid., 301–2.

[29] According to one source, initially there was a limited amount of support for the infiltrators in Batmaloo, a *mohalla* (neighborhood) of Srinagar. The welcome, however, quickly wore off as the infiltrators increased their demands on the local populace. (Personal communication with Professor Amitabh Mattoo, Jawaharlal Nehru University, March 26, 1996.)

[30] Brines, *The Indo-Pakistani Conflict*, 319–21.

state within the Indian Union and also saw the arrest and exile to southern India of Sheikh Abdullah. Yet these events and the Hazratbal episode produced only limited unrest in the valley. More to the point, not even when Pakistan made overt attempts to provoke the Kashmiris into acting against the Indian state did the local population rise up.

Thus, the historical evidence suggests that neither of the two explanations presented at the beginning of this chapter is sufficient. The evidence simply does not support the view that Pakistani apologists have propagated. Segments of Kashmir's population did have real and imagined grievances against the government of India in general and its toleration of the corrupt Bakshi regime in particular. These grievances could, as the demonstrations in the wake of the Hazratbal episode showed, be successfully mobilized. However, they did not amount to a secessionist movement based along ethnoreligious lines. It is also true that a section of Kashmiri Muslim opinion did favor merger with Pakistan. But clearly this did not represent the view of all Muslim Kashmiris, let alone all Kashmiris.

The opposite explanation, namely that Pakistani instigation of an existing disaffection among a minority of Kashmiris could cause a secessionist insurgency, is equally false. Ample evidence of Pakistan's attempt to systematically organize, train, arm, and then infiltrate guerrillas into the Kashmir valley has been presented. Despite this well-orchestrated effort, the result was a complete failure. The Kashmiris simply failed to respond in the manner expected.

The historical evidence challenges both explanations. The Kashmiris, despite their grievances, did not spontaneously mobilize around a shared belief in a collective Muslim identity that was under siege. Even a fairly obvious catalyst, the Hazratbal episode, could not provide the impetus for generating an ethnoreligious movement. Pakistan's attempts to stoke these grievances also failed. The explanation for the mobilization of grievances against the Indian state needs to be found elsewhere.

4

Another war and
Mrs. Gandhi's legacy

In 1971 India and Pakistan went to war for the third time since 1947, but this time they did not go to war over Kashmir.[1] In response to increased demands for autonomy in East Pakistan (now Bangladesh), the Pakistani army had begun a brutal crackdown in Dacca (now Dhaka), the capital of East Pakistan, in late March 1971. After several thousand East Pakistanis had been killed, close to 10 million refugees began streaming across the border into the Indian state of West Bengal. This influx placed an extraordinary burden on India. When several attempts to focus the concern of the international community on the situation in East Pakistan and on the plight of the refugees failed to produce a diplomatic solution that would be acceptable to the East Pakistani leadership and that would ensure the return of the refugees, the Indian political leadership under Prime Minister Indira Gandhi decided that it was cheaper to go to war than to absorb the refugees into India's population.

Accordingly, the government's foreign-intelligence arm, the Research and Analysis Wing, in concert with the army and paramilitary forces, particularly the Border Security Force, began to organize, train, and provide sanctuary to the indigenous guerrilla

---

[1] For a more detailed presentation of the tactics and strategies of the 1971 Indo-Pakistani war, see Šumit Ganguly, "Wars without End? The Indo-Pakistani Conflict," *Annals of the American Academy of Political and Social Science* 541 (September 1995): 167–78.

inclination to stir up trouble in Kashmir. Under these circumstances the Pakistani leadership was more inclined to focus on domestic priorities and not to undertake yet another foreign misadventure in the region. Prime Minister Zulfiquar Ali Bhutto, in fact, consciously sought to redirect Pakistan's foreign policy toward the Islamic Middle East, particularly toward Iran.[5]

Third, there was little or no opportunity for Pakistan to exploit the situation in Kashmir. During the 1971 war, Kashmir had been the site of a handful of pitched battles. India had two major military objectives in Kashmir and the western front: to destroy as much Pakistani armor and military hardware as possible and to capture and hold any strategic salients along the CFL in Kashmir.[6] The Indian military accomplished both these objectives without much difficulty. The local population of the Kashmir valley, as in 1965, cooperated with the Indian forces. Even if any discontent had existed in the valley, it did not redound to Pakistan's advantage.

Fourth, the Simla Agreement, which was signed in 1972, reflected this altered military and power relationship on the subcontinent. One of India's long-standing concerns was finally addressed in the Simla Agreement. Under the aegis of the accord, the two sides "resolved to settle their differences by peaceful means through *bilateral negotiations* or by any other peaceful means mutually agreed upon between them."[7] The mention of bilateral negotiations is significant. Since India's ill-fated experience of taking the Kashmir dispute to the United Nations, successive Indian governments had made every effort to limit third-party or multilateral initiatives for settling the Kashmir question. Pakistan, as the weaker state in the region, had sought to do precisely the opposite. It had consistently sought to internationalize the dispute and had enlisted the support of various nations to bolster its position.

[5] Marin Weinbaum and Gautam Sen, "Pakistan Enters the Middle East," *Orbis* 22:3 (Fall 1978): 595–612.
[6] The best description and analysis of Indian goals in the Kashmir sector of the Western front during the 1971 war can be found in Chopra, *India's Second Liberation*.
[7] See paragraph two of the Simla Agreement, in Appendix 4 (emphasis added).

The Simla Agreement's explicit recognition of the principle of bilateralism in Indo-Pakistani relations was widely construed in Indian policy-making circles as a major diplomatic victory.[8]

THE LIMITS OF INDIAN DIPLOMACY

Indira Gandhi and her coterie of foreign policy advisers, most notably D. P. Dhar, chairman of the Policy Planning Committee in the Ministry of External Affairs, P. N. Haksar, principal secretary to the prime minister, P. N. Dhar, secretary to the prime minister, and T. N. Kaul, foreign secretary, proved quite skillful in translating India's military victory into diplomatic triumphs. As Pran Chopra, an eminent Indian journalist, commented on the accord in 1974:

> The subcontinent is not only bound to a peace treaty now, but there are means available within the subcontinent for enforcing the treaty by making its violation extremely expensive. This is a position which India had sought for the best part of two decades; now, at last, she has been able to get it, and more or less on her own terms.[9]

Nevertheless the Indian politicians were unsuccessful in accomplishing one key objective. Despite considerable cajolery and arm-twisting, the Indian negotiators were unable to obtain Bhutto's acquiescence on transforming the Line of Control (LOC) into a permanent, de jure international border.[10] According to P. N. Dhar, writing in April 1995, Bhutto had agreed at Simla, in

[8]   A thoughtful analysis of the Simla Agreement can be found in Imtiaz H. Bokhari and Thomas Perry Thornton, *The 1972 Simla Agreement: An Asymmetrical Negotiation* (Washington, D.C.: Foreign Policy Institute, Johns Hopkins School of Advanced International Studies, 1988).

[9]   Chopra, *India's Second Liberation,* 250.

[10] It is important to mention that the Indian side had tried this earlier, in 1963, in the sixth and final round of talks with Pakistan on Kashmir, only to be rebuffed by Bhutto. See M. J. Akbar, *Kashmir: Behind the Vale* (New Delhi: Viking, 1991), 175. Also see A. G. Noorani, "Kashmir: The Lost Opportunity," *Illustrated Weekly of India,* September 7, 1986, 50–53.

principle, to convert the LOC into an international border. However, he contended that as the leader of the defeated state, he could ill afford to take the political risks associated with such a public stance. Furthermore, he argued that Pakistan had just emerged from fourteen years of military rule. He was just beginning to consolidate democratic rule. A momentous concession on the highly emotive Kashmir issue could well lead to his ouster. Finally, Bhutto also pointed to divisions within his own delegation. In effect, he insisted that after sufficient time had passed and the passions of the military debacle had subsided in Pakistan, he would be willing to return to the matter. His Indian interlocutors reluctantly agreed to wait.[11] In the 1990s, following the outbreak of the insurgency in Kashmir and Pakistan's efforts to focus renewed international attention on the Kashmir dispute, many Indian commentators sharply criticized the Indian failure at Simla to press the status of the border.[12]

Subsequent political developments in Pakistan increasingly drew Bhutto's attention away from Kashmir. Initially, he concentrated on the problems of a new (1973) constitution for Pakistan. Later, the efforts to suppress an insurgency in Baluchistan and to contain ethnic violence in Sind preoccupied his regime. Furthermore, Bhutto made a conscious attempt to direct Pakistan's foreign policy orientation toward the Middle East. With the quadrupling of oil prices in 1973 in the wake of the third Arab-Israeli conflict, relations with the Arab Middle East states and Iran became important concerns for Pakistan.[13]

This shift in Pakistan's foreign policy concerns and priorities also coincided with India's brief sense of euphoria as the emergent great power in the region. Consequently, the Indian leadership was content to leave the Kashmir issue untouched.

[11] Author interview with senior Indian diplomat, New York, April 1993. See also P. N. Dhar, "LOC as Border: Bhutto's Deal with Mrs. Gandhi," *Times of India*, April 4, 1995, and Abdul Sattar, "Simla Pact: Negotiation under Duress;" *Regional Studies* 13:4 (Autumn 1995): 28–45.

[12] See, for example, Ajit Bhattacharjea, *Kashmir: The Wounded Valley* (New Delhi: UBSPD, 1994).

[13] Weinbaum and Sen, "Pakistan Enters the Middle East."

THE OTHER SIDE OF SIMLA:
DEVELOPMENTS IN THE VALE

The Indian leadership did not demonstrate dexterity in dealing with the domestic politics of Kashmir in the wake of the Simla Agreement. After the agreement, Indira Gandhi did focus on the question of Kashmir's position within the Indian Union. But the exigencies of domestic politics, combined with Gandhi's personal predilections, worked against any meaningful efforts by the national government to establish a more durable relationship with the Kashmiris.

Two interrelated factors can be adduced to explain the eventual failure to reach a more lasting solution to the domestic dimensions of the Kashmir problem. First, after 1971 Indira Gandhi's personal popularity was at its zenith. Even her most ardent and strident critics were willing to concede that she had demonstrated extraordinary political acumen in resolving the 1971 crisis.[14] Despite this overwhelming level of personal popularity, however, she remained a deeply insecure leader.[15] In many ways this personal insecurity led her to systematically denude every institution in the Indian polity.[16]

What relevance did this particular proclivity have for the Kashmir problem? The vast majority of Kashmir's Muslims had amply demonstrated their loyalty to India during both the 1965 and the 1971 wars. There was little reason to believe that separatist politics would make significant headway despite the formation of the

[14] See Shashi Tharoor, *Reasons of State* (New Delhi: Vikas, 1982).

[15] The best analysis of Indira Gandhi's political personality and its impact on India's politics and political culture can be found in Henry Hart, ed., *Indira Gandhi's India: A Political System Re-appraised* (Boulder: Westview, 1980).

[16] For an insightful discussion, see James Manor, "The Dynamics of Political Integration and Disintegration," in *The States of South Asia: Problems of National Integration,* ed. A. Jeyaratnam Wilson and Dennis Dalton (Honolulu: University of Hawaii Press, 1982). For a broad treatment of the subject, see Paul R. Brass, *The Politics of India since Independence,* 2d ed. (Cambridge: Cambridge University Press, 1994).

Jammu and Kashmir Liberation Front (JKLF).[17] Yet Gandhi had considerable difficulty allowing the emergence of any autonomous organization that might challenge the supremacy of the Congress Party, in Kashmir or elsewhere.

Second, as a consequence of her proclivity to aggrandize power in New Delhi, even accords with local leaders were frequently not implemented in letter or spirit. One such agreement, the Beg-Parthasarathi Accord, which should have restored a modicum of autonomy to Kashmir, fell prey to Gandhi's refusal to promote any degree of genuine federalism. The complex and tortured negotiations that led up to the Beg-Parthasarathi Accord, which paved the way for Sheikh Abdullah's return to power in Kashmir, will demonstrate the validity of the propositions noted above.

THE RETURN OF THE LION AND "THE QUANTUM OF AUTONOMY"

During the 1971 war, a Kashmiri political activist and journalist, Balraj Puri, suggested to Sheikh Abdullah that he explicitly support Indira Gandhi's Bangladesh policy. Initially, the sheikh, who was prohibited under an administrative order from entering Kashmir, was willing to give his support. However, at the behest of his lieutenant, Mirza Afzal Beg, he decided against it.[18] Subsequently, Puri met with both Indira Gandhi and Sheikh Abdullah in December 1971. Even before any discussions ensued about a new dispensation between the state of Kashmir and the Indian Union, Abdullah started to insist on returning Kashmir to its pre-1952 status.[19] (At that time, the government of India had control over only three key aspects of Kashmir's governance—defense, foreign affairs, and

---

[17] The Jammu and Kashmir Liberation Front is the oldest, notionally secular, proindependence movement in the Kashmir valley. It was formed in the wake of the 1965 Indo-Pakistani conflict.

[18] Author interview with Balraj Puri, Washington, D.C., March 10, 1994.

[19] Sheikh Abdullah's letter to G. Parthasarathi, as reprinted in Abdul Jabbar Ganai, *Kashmir and National Conference, and Politics, 1975–1980* (Srinagar: Gulshan, 1984).

communications.) Such preconditions were fundamentally unacceptable to the vast majority of the Indian cabinet and certainly to Indira Gandhi.[20] If any negotiations were to take place, the gulf between the two parties first had to be significantly narrowed. Accordingly, Puri suggested to Sheikh Abdullah that he would be in a far better position to press his demands if he initially acquired a mantle of legitimacy. This, Puri contended, could best be accomplished if Abdullah sought the chief ministership of the state. Unfortunately, Abdullah could not be persuaded to run unless his preconditions were met.

State assembly elections were declared on February 5, 1972. The principal leaders of the Plebiscite Front, Mirza Afzal Beg, Maulana Masoodi, and Ghulam Mohiuddin Karra, would not agree to language acceptable to the government of India in their party election manifesto, which insisted on severing allegiance to the Indian Constitution. Consequently, they were prohibited from taking part in the elections.[21] The Congress(I) Party (born out of the split in the Congress Party in 1969) came to power in the assembly, and Syed Mir Qasim, a former head of the Pradesh Congress of Jammu and Kashmir, became chief minister. Out of a total of seventy-five assembly seats, the Congress won fifty-seven, the Jammat-i-Islami five, the Jana Sangh (the forerunner to today's Bharatiya Janata Party) three, the National Conference one, and the independent candidates the remaining nine. Several of the members of the opposition were known to be sympathizers of the Plebiscite Front. Only after they swore allegiance to both the Indian *and* the Kashmiri constitutions were they allowed to take their seats in the Kashmir Legislative Assembly.

After Gandhi's refusal to budge on Kashmir, Sheikh Abdullah became disconsolate. At one point, in a burst of emotional fury, he is reported to have declared, "Throw my body in the Arabian Sea—do not bury me in a slave country." Balraj Puri nevertheless continued to urge the sheikh to start discussions with Indira Gandhi. Eventually, the sheikh agreed, and he wrote to her insisting

[20] Mir Qasim, *My Life and Times* (New Delhi: Allied, 1992), 137–8.
[21] Bhattacharjea, *Kashmir*, 230.

that all he was concerned with was "the quantum of autonomy" that could be obtained for Kashmir.[22] This letter finally paved the way for discussions between G. Parthasarathi, a senior Indian bureaucrat and Gandhi loyalist, and Mirza Afzal Beg, one of Abdullah's most trusted acolytes.

The negotiations culminated with Beg making most of the concessions. To begin with, Abdullah and Beg had to concede that the Instrument of Accession as ratified by the Jammu and Kashmir Assembly under Bakshi Ghulam Mohammed was no longer subject to challenge. Thus, the debates over the plebiscite to determine the future of Kashmir effectively were quashed outright. In return, Beg sought to extend the Fundamental Rights provisions of the Indian Constitution to the Jammu and Kashmir Constitution, asked for the removal of the authority of the national Election Commission over Kashmir, and insisted on modifications in Article 356 of the Indian Constitution to ensure that President's Rule could not be arbitrarily imposed on Kashmir.[23] Parthasarathi, at Indira Gandhi's insistence, would not budge on any of these issues. The best that Beg could obtain was to keep Article 370 intact.[24] He also exacted a promise that the state government could review a number of legislative acts of the Indian Parliament since 1953 pertaining to Kashmir.[25]

Despite the continuation of Article 370, the accord brought about a number of changes in the relationship between Jammu

[22] Author interview with Balraj Puri, Washington, D.C., March 10, 1994.

[23] Akbar, *Kashmir,* 187. The declaration of President's Rule allows the central government to take over the administration of a state following either the dismissal or the collapse of the elected state government.

[24] Article 370 of the Indian Constitution ensures, among other things, that non-Kashmiris cannot purchase immovable property in the state. Thus the demography of the state cannot be altered through migration and settlement. For a discussion of the significance of Article 370, see S. P. Sathe, "Article 370: Constitutional Obligations and Compulsions," in *Secular Crown on Fire: The Kashmir Problem,* ed. Asghar Ali Engineer (Delhi: Ajanta, 1991). Article 370 can be found in Appendix 2.

[25] For an informed, if recondite, analysis of Article 370, see Mohan Krishen Teng, *Kashmir Article 370* (New Delhi: Anmol, 1990). The full text of the Beg-Parthasarathi Accord is reprinted in Ganai, *Kashmir.*

and Kashmir and the central government. Specifically, it gave the president of India the right to review certain legislative acts of the Jammu and Kashmir assembly before they became law. This clause in the accord primarily dealt with legislation in the areas pertaining to the functions of the governor of the state and to a number of issues related to elections.[26]

The failure by India to fashion a more durable relationship with Kashmir at this juncture amounted to a vital lost opportunity. As one noted Indian journalist has written:

> In Kashmir, however, the impact of Pakistan's defeat and the separation of Bangladesh was far-reaching. Those who wanted to join Pakistan realized that it did not have the strength to force the issue. Those wanting independence found that Pakistan was not playing an effective counterpoise to India and the scope for playing one against the other was exhausted. Besides, the emergence of Bangladesh demonstrated that ethnic pulls could be stronger than religious ties.[27]

FROM PLEBISCITE FRONT TO NATIONAL CONFERENCE

The plebiscitary phase in Kashmir's politics drew to a close with the Beg-Parthasarathi Accord. Abdullah essentially agreed to put an end to his political oscillation in return for his accession to the chief ministership of Kashmir. Accordingly, on July 5, 1975, his breakaway party, the All Jammu and Kashmir Plebiscite Front, folded itself into the National Conference.

Abdullah's accession to power in Kashmir did not resolve the continuing tussle between the Congress(I) government of Indira Gandhi and the National Conference regime in the state, however. The Congress(I) organization within Kashmir continued to demand greater representation in the state assembly. Sheikh Abdullah and the National Conference called on the Congress(I) to fold its organization into the ranks of the National Conference. This

[26] See Article 5 of the Beg-Parthasarathi Accord, in Ganai, *Kashmir.*
[27] Bhattacharjea, *Kashmir,* 233.

was clearly unacceptable to the Pradesh Congress (local Congress) command.

Even though these squabbles with the Congress(I) consumed his energies, Sheikh Abdullah did make efforts to improve the quality of the administration in the state. For example, he instituted reforms that involved steps to nominate public representatives to District Development Boards, with the eventual goal of having elected representatives. In many ways these reforms were an important precursor of the central government's efforts, a decade later, to strengthen Panchayati Raj (local self-government).[28]

Abdullah also attempted to stem the decline in state facilities. More funds were allocated for building and repairing educational institutions, and efforts were also undertaken to quell widespread student indiscipline. Various plans for improving tourist facilities and state infrastructure were also sanctioned.

The political tussle between the state-level Congress(I) and the National Conference continued to dog Abdullah's rule. In March 1977 the leader of the Congress(I), Mufti Mohammed Sayeed, decided to withdraw his party's support from the Abdullah–National Conference coalition. The Congress(I) had as many as forty-six seats in the seventy-six-seat assembly. It also succeeded in persuading five members of the Jammat-i-Islami Party to withdraw support from the Abdullah regime. This combination left Sheikh Abdullah with little or no backing within the assembly. Having decided to bring down the regime, Mufti Sayeed requested that the governor, the economist and former diplomat L. K. Jha, dissolve the assembly and permit him, as the leader of the majority party in the assembly, to form a government. Abdullah got wind of Sayeed's scheme and promptly contacted the governor. Abdullah also proposed the dissolution of the assembly but simultaneously called for fresh elections. The governor chose to dissolve the assembly and call for new elections. In the interim, President's Rule was imposed on Jammu and Kashmir on March 27, 1977, and elections were scheduled for June 1977.

[28] Author interview with senior Indian government official, New Delhi, August 1995.

Abdullah chose this opportunity to try to free himself from the clutches of the Congress(I). In the March 1977 national election, the Congress(I) had been resoundingly defeated—the many draconian measures that had been enacted under Indira Gandhi's eighteen-month "emergency" rule had alienated much of India's electorate.[29] A new coalition regime under the banner of the Janata Party had come to power. Accordingly, Abdullah systematically went about courting key members of the Janata regime.[30] However, he was not prepared to merge the National Conference with Janata. In any event, Janata decided to create a unit of its own in Jammu and Kashmir. In the post-"emergency" euphoria, many prominent Kashmiri political leaders decided to throw in their lot with Janata. When a socialist leader of long standing, Asoka Mehta, decided to set up Janata's organizational base in Jammu and Kashmir, he received the assistance of veteran Kashmiri politicians like Maulana Mohammed Syed Masoodi (who became the convener of the Janata in the valley) and Ghulam Mohiuddin Karra. Even erstwhile pro-plebiscite leaders like Mirwaiz Mohammed Farooq, the chair of the Kashmiri Awami Action Committee, decided to back the Janata Party.[31]

At a national level, the idiosyncratic prime minister, Morarji Desai, personally visited Kashmir to reiterate his commitment to a free and fair election. Other Janata Party leaders, including Chaudhury Charan Singh and Babu Jagjivan Ram, echoed Desai's sentiments at various preelection rallies in Srinagar.

When the elections were held on June 3, the National Conference won handsomely. It obtained an overwhelming majority in the assembly, winning forty-seven of a possible seventy-six elective seats in the state. The Congress(I) secured eleven. The Janata Party won thirteen seats. The communal party, the Jammat-i-Islami, was effectively marginalized, winning one seat. Various independents won the remaining four. It is interesting to note that not a single

[29] Hart, *Indira Gandhi's India.*
[30] Prem Nath Bazaz, *Democracy through Intimidation and Terror* (New Delhi: Heritage, 1978), 38–9.
[31] Ibid., 53.

Congress(I) politician won a seat in the Kashmir valley. In part, this was due to a lackluster campaign in the wake of its national electoral rout.

With marked exceptions, virtually all political observers regard this election as the most free and fair election that had ever been conducted in the state of Jammu and Kashmir.[32] As Balraj Puri wrote in 1981, "A quantum jump in the process of political and emotional re-integration of Kashmir with the rest of India took place in what have been universally acknowledged as the fairest and freest elections to the State Assembly in 1977."[33] Yet in a remarkably prescient fashion, Puri provided a warning:

> It would nevertheless be rash to conclude that Indian federalisation in Jammu and Kashmir State is complete and perfect. It can receive a set-back in any part of the country and the State is in no way an exception. In fact there is hardly any federal set-up in the world that is permanently and completely immune from potential troubles.[34]

The popular mandate that Abdullah received should have ushered in a new era both in the governance of the state and in center-state relations. Unfortunately, through a variety of factors, neither transpired. Abdullah, never a staunch democrat, was not above using democratic procedures for more parochial ends. After the 1977 elections, the National Conference was firmly ensconced. Within months of coming to power, in November 1977, Abdullah's government passed the Jammu and Kashmir Safety Ordinance, which placed severe restrictions on newspapers and other publications within the state in the interests of security and public

---

[32] Sumanto Banerjee, "Redefining Integration," *Seminar*, April 1992, 32–6. Also see Balraj Puri, *Kashmir: Towards Insurgency* (New Delhi: Orient Longman, 1993). A sharply contrasting view can be found in Bazaz, *Democracy through Intimidation*. Bazaz, who had associated himself with the Janata Party's Ad Hoc Committee in Jammu and Kashmir, accuses Sheikh Abdullah and the National Conference of a series of electoral malfeasances. Among other matters, he charges that Abdullah raised the specter of a Janata regime that would abolish Article 370.

[33] Balraj Puri, *Triumph and Tragedy of Indian Federalisation* (New Delhi: Sterling, 1981), 189.

[34] Ibid., 191.

order. Ostensibly, this ordinance was necessary to tackle Pakistani-sponsored subversive activity in the state.[35] Understandably, newspapers both within Kashmir and at the national level criticized the ordinance. The Janata government also chided the Abdullah regime for this blatant attempt to stifle civil liberties. The timing of the ordinance was laden with considerable irony. The country had recently emerged from the harrowing experience of the eighteen-month State of Emergency, when Indira Gandhi, in the name of national security, had systematically squelched personal rights and civil liberties.

Faced with concerted opposition, Abdullah removed some of the more objectionable features of the ordinance but refused to abandon it altogether. Worse still, within a few months he decided to move legislation in the state assembly to make the ordinance a legal statute. On April 1, 1978, Deputy Chief Minister Mirza Afzal Beg introduced the Public Safety Bill in the state assembly. The reaction of both the press and the opposition was entirely predictable. Most newspapers denounced the bill in stark terms. Abdul Ghani Lone, the leader of the opposition, referred to the bill as a "black law."[36] Yet the pleas and criticisms had little impact on Abdullah and the National Conference. With its numerical majority, the ruling party was easily able to drive the bill through the legislature.

It is not entirely clear what short-term gains this piece of legislation achieved. It is quite clear in retrospect, however, that the passage of this law effectively closed yet another avenue for the airing of political grievances at the local level. It can be argued that in 1978 Sheikh Abdullah no longer had an adequate appreciation of the changes in the political culture of the state. A new generation of educated, politicized, and more articulate Kashmiris had begun to emerge during his long years of political exile. As Prem Nath Bazaz has correctly argued,

---

[35] The details of the ordinance are discussed in Bazaz, *Democracy through Intimidation*, 152–4.

[36] Ibid., 186.

Tremendous changes had taken place in and outside Jammu and Kashmir. The educated Muslim youth whose number multiplied several times in 30 years realized that Sheikh Abdullah's inconsistent behaviour had done immense harm to the interests of the Kashmiris; it had thwarted their progress and deprived them of several political and human rights enjoyed by all the other Indians.[37]

The full impact of Abdullah's malfeasances, as well as those of the central government, would be felt by the end of the decade.

Abdullah's propensity to centralize decision making also led to another turbulent episode in the political life of Kashmir in September 1978. G. M. Shah, the sheikh's son-in-law, harbored aspirations of becoming his heir. Accordingly, Shah embarked on a campaign of ostracizing and slighting Beg. Over time a rift developed between the two men. The sheikh's son Farooq Abdullah, to his credit, did much to bring about some reconciliation between the two men shortly before Beg died. Nevertheless, Shah remained unreconciled to the sheikh's decision to name his son Farooq as his successor.

THE EMERGENCE OF A NEW GENERATION

Despite Abdullah's ability for deft political maneuver, he was incapable of controlling certain sociopolitical forces that were at work in the state. His network of political patronage and clientelism could not contain and absorb the percolation of Islamic sentiment, which stemmed largely from four sources.

The first source presents a paradox. The limited success of the central government in promoting economic development in the state ironically helped alienate younger Kashmiris. The central government in New Delhi had allocated significant resources to Kashmir through a succession of National Conference regimes. Sheikh Abdullah's regime, in particular, had been an important beneficiary of the central government's largesse since his return to

[37] Ibid., 161.

Table 4.1. *Sources of revenue for Jammu and Kashmir, 1950–88*

	Percentage of state's total revenue coming from:	
Year	State resources	National government
1950–1	96.28	3.71
1960–1	70.80	29.20
1970–1	43.71	56.29
1980–1	31.57	68.43
1987–8	27.95	72.04

Source: Afsir Karim and the Indian Defence Review Team, *Kashmir: The Troubled Frontiers* (New Delhi: Lancers, 1994), 242.

power in 1975 (see, for example, Table 4.1).[38] The resources devoted to the state did improve the material standards of the Kashmiri populace; dispassionate observers have commented on the tremendous economic transformation produced in the region.[39] However, this process in itself set off other expectations and demands. Young Kashmiris acquired a modicum of education and became aware of improved economic prospects. They were no longer content to seek employment in the traditional sectors of the economy, namely, the handicraft industry or the tourist trade. The National Conference did little to expand employment growth in new sectors of the economy. Inevitably, a reservoir of discontent grew among the quasi-educated and largely prospectless youth of the Kashmir valley.

The economic transformation of the valley had other unanticipated social consequences that also created a climate conducive to the growth of radical Islamic sentiment. Earlier in the decade,

[38] This point requires clarification. Contrary to popular belief, Kashmir did not have the highest per capita central investment. Furthermore, the loan and aid portions of the plan were quite skewed. Consequently, much of the plan expenditure was diverted to debt servicing. (Author interview with Jammu and Kashmir state government economist, New Delhi, January 1995.)

[39] On this point, see Phillips Talbot, "Kashmir's Agony," in *India Briefing 1990*, ed. Philip Oldenburg (Boulder: Westview, 1991).

in the neighboring state of Punjab, the uneven rewards and the dislocative effects of the "Green Revolution" had contributed to the rise of revitalist sentiment among sections of the Sikh community.[40] Young, wealthy, urbanized Sikhs had sought to shear off the trappings of their faith. Among the more conservative sections of the Sikh community, such behavior had reinvigorated a concern that they could well become absorbed within the Hindu fold.[41] This anxiety in turn was one of the major precipitants of the rise of revitalistic sentiment in the state.[42]

In Kashmir, a modicum of economic growth and the expansion of secondary and college education produced some of the same effects. Economic development produced a fitful social transformation of the valley. One indicator of this transformation of mores was the dramatic growth and popularity of video parlors, catering to a variety of tastes, throughout the small towns of the valley.[43]

Interestingly enough, as in the Punjab, the growth of the *madrassas* (Islamic schools) paralleled the expansion of the video parlors. Unlike the Sikhs in the Punjab, however, the lower-middle-class Muslims of the valley had little fear of being absorbed into Hinduism. Yet they did find shifts in social mores disturbing. These changes in norms and values no doubt explain the growth of the *madrassas*. In the emerging milieu, where traditional values were eroding, those most threatened sought solace in a form of revitalistic Islam.[44]

The second, idiosyncratic source, rooted in India's domestic politics, also explains the dramatic and abrupt growth in the

[40] Šumit Ganguly, "Ethno-Religious Conflict in South Asia," *Survival* 35:2 (Summer 1993): 88–109.

[41] Rajiv Kapur, *Sikh Separatism: The Politics of Faith* (London: Allen and Unwin, 1986).

[42] The two classic statements on revitalistic movements are Ralph Linton, "Nativistic Movements," *American Anthropologist* 45 (January–March 1943): 231–41, and Anthony C. F. Wallace, "Revitalization Movements," *American Anthropologist* 58:2 (April 1956): 264–81.

[43] Many of the video parlors made pornographic movies widely available. I am indebted to Amitabh Mattoo of Jawaharlal Nehru University for a thoughtful discussion of this subject.

[44] Bhattacharjea, *Kashmir*, 238–9.

number of the *madrassas*. As was mentioned in Chapter 2, in 1983 the vast majority of the Muslim residents of Nellie, a village in Assam, were massacred on the eve of a state-level election. The immediate precipitant of this systematic ethnic violence was the growing anxiety of the native Assamese about illegal immigration from predominantly Muslim Bangladesh. In the wake of this massacre substantial numbers of Assamese Muslims fled to Kashmir. Among the migrants were Muslim clergy who had become convinced that they had little future in India. Many of them were employed as *maulvis* (religious teachers) in the *madrassas*. In the absence of systematic data, definitive conclusions about their impact on the ethnoreligious sentiments of Kashmiri youth are difficult to ascertain. Nevertheless, the entry of these Muslim migrants most likely spurred the development of a new brand of ethnoreligious sentiment directed against the Indian state.

The organizational structure of the National Conference was the third source contributing to the search for alternative avenues of expressing socioeconomic discontent. Why did the National Conference not serve as an outlet for the growing body of discontent within the valley? We have already commented on the tight hold that Sheikh Abdullah maintained on the National Conference. His organizational style limited the prospects of dissent from its precepts and practices. This form of party organization certainly discouraged new and more obstreperous entrants into the party's ranks. Paradoxically, the one redeeming feature of the National Conference was the sheikh's towering leadership. His long involvement in Kashmiri politics, his years of opposition to the maharaja's rule before independence, and his oratorical skills helped sustain his tenacious popularity among the Kashmiri people.[45]

The fourth source has to be sought in the changing regional sociocultural context of the time, particularly within Pakistan. In an attempt to weaken the power of the *mullahs*, President Zia-

[45] See Puri, *Kashmir*, 43.

ul-Haq of Pakistan had embarked on an extensive, if cosmetic, Islamicization program in Pakistan. Domestically, it involved the development of parallel Islamic courts based on the *shariat* (Islamic law).[46] At a regional level, it involved concerted support for the fundamentalist elements of the Afghan *mujahideen*. One of the principal benefactors of Zia-ul-Haq's largesse was Gulubuddin Hekmatayar of the Hezb-ul-Islami guerrilla group. Later, particularly as the war in Afghanistan started to wind down, Zia's attention was directed toward the growing sense of disenchantment within the Kashmir valley. One branch of this stream of discontent gathered volume and flowed in the direction of Islamic radicalism. Accordingly, General Zia-ul-Haq used the Pakistani army's powerful Inter-Service Intelligence (ISI) organization to fund, organize, and train young, disaffected Kashmiris imbued with recently discovered Islamic fervor to challenge the writ of the Indian state.[47]

The peculiar conjunction of these four sources contributed to the rise of Islamic fundamentalism in the Kashmir valley. It is important and pertinent to note that fundamentalist Islam was previously unknown in the region. The physical isolation of the valley and the long-standing presence of Hindus in the midst of a

---

[46] Charles H. Kennedy, "Islamicization in Pakistan," *Asian Survey* 28:3 (March 1988): 307–16. See also Riaz Hassan, "Religion, Society, and the State in Pakistan," *Asian Survey* 27:5 (May 1987): 552–66.

[47] For evidence of Pakistan's active support for the insurgency and the ISI's involvement, see "Kashmir: Conspiracy Theory," *Economist*, July 13, 1991, 35–6; R. A. Davis, "Kashmir in the Balance," *International Defense Review* 4 (1991): 301–4; and Edward W. Desmond, "Pakistan's Hidden Hand," *Time*, July 22, 1991, 23. See also Chris Smith, *The Diffusion of Small Arms and Light Weapons in Pakistan and Northern India* (London: Brassey's, 1993), and John Ward Anderson, "Pakistan Aiding Rebels in Kashmir," *Washington Post*, May 16, 1994, A12–A13. For a discussion of how the failure of secular regimes to promote economic development and social justice has given rise to Islamic fundamentalist movements in the Middle East and Central Asia, see Mark Juergensmeyer, *The New Cold War? Religious Nationalism Confronts the Secular State* (Berkeley: University of California Press, 1993).

predominantly Muslim population had produced a variant of Islam that had little or nothing in common with the various other branches of South Asian Islam.[48]

One of the manifestations of this rise in Islamic fervor was the threat of the Jammat-i-Islami Party and its youth wing, the Jammat-i-Tulba, to launch an "Iran-type" movement to "liberate" Kashmir from India.[49] Neither Sheikh Abdullah's government nor the central government in New Delhi took this threat lightly. Almost immediately after this announcement, on August 7, 1980, the state police, in a night-long sweep, arrested some twenty-four leaders connected with the Jammat. These tough and swift measures did limit the activities of these organizations; however, the underlying conditions that had spawned the movements remained largely unaddressed.[50]

THE POLITICS OF THE RESETTLEMENT BILL

Abdullah's propensity for political chicanery caused further turbulence in the state. In March 1980, no doubt with an eye directed toward silencing those critics who had chastised him for Kashmir's full accession to India, Abdullah introduced in the Jammu and Kashmir Legislative Assembly a bill that could best be described as a populist measure. This piece of legislation, known as the Resettlement Bill, was ostensibly designed to facilitate the return of those Kashmiri residents who had fled the state during the upheaval of 1947. Notionally, the purpose of the bill was to

[48] See G. M. D. Sufi, *Islamic Culture in Kashmir* (New Delhi: Light and Life, 1979). It also needs to be noted that Islam came to Kashmir not as a conquering, imperial faith but through the activities of Sufi mendicants in the fourteenth century.

[49] "Police Crush Revolt of Kashmiri Secessionists," Foreign Broadcast Information Service, Near East and South Asia (FBIS-NES), August 7, 1980.

[50] Some acute observers of Kashmiri politics have argued that the sheikh's relationship with the Jammat was complex. The sheikh manipulated the Jammat to suit his own ends. On occasion he would encourage the Jammat to instill fear in New Delhi. He was also quite capable of repressing the party when it suited his own ends. (Author interview with a senior Indian government official, New York, March 1995.)

provide a legal basis and a set of procedures to enable pre-1947 residents to return to the state.[51] Specifically, the legislation gave any Kashmiri who had been a state subject before May 14, 1954, or a descendant of the subject, the right to return to Kashmir as long as the individual swore allegiance to the Constitution of India and the Constitution of Jammu and Kashmir.[52]

The most obvious criticism of this bill was that it would endanger the security of the state. Kashmiris who had migrated to Pakistan in 1947 and were now Pakistani citizens could well be recruited as agents provocateurs and sent into the valley. The issue became especially sensitive when General Krishna Rao, the chief of staff of the Indian army, publicly stated that the passage and implementation of the bill could create serious national security problems for India.[53] In a country in which the tradition of civil-military relations precludes senior military commanders from publicly making political pronouncements, General Rao's statement was most unusual.

At the level of regional politics, the bill also provoked sharp reactions, particularly in Jammu. Hindu and Sikh refugees who had resettled on property that had once belonged to Muslims now felt threatened. Abdullah insisted, however, that proper procedures for vetting individual applicants would be established. Eventually, the state assembly passed the bill in 1982. In September 1982 the governor, Braj Kumar Nehru, returned the bill to the legislature for reconsideration.

The bill's initial passage was one of the sheikh's final acts in office. On September 8, 1982, Sheikh Mohammed Abdullah passed away. Before his death, in August 1981, he had anointed his political heir—his son Farooq Abdullah, a medical doctor who had been in private practice in London.[54]

---

[51] Narinder Singh, *Political Awakening in Kashmir* (Delhi: H. K. Publications, 1992), 158.
[52] Akbar, *Kashmir*, 197.
[53] Agence France Presse Hong Kong, June 5, 1982, as reported in FBIS-NES, June 8, 1982.
[54] Farooq had already been made the head of the National Conference.

Despite the political chicanery that he had engaged in on many occasions, there is little question that Sheikh Abdullah remained extraordinarily popular among Kashmiris until his death. The valley exhibited an outpouring of mourning as his body lay in state on a specially constructed platform on the Polo Grounds in Srinagar.[55]

ENTER FAROOQ ABDULLAH

Farooq Abdullah was a complete political neophyte. Unlike his father, who had earned his political credentials as early as the 1930s in his opposition to Maharaja Hari Singh, Farooq knew little or nothing about the rough-and-tumble world of Kashmir's politics. Moreover, he lacked his father's substantial organizational skills. Above all, his brief and infelicitous first stint in office suggests that he came to power with little inclination for tackling the serious problems of political office.

In a socially conservative state, Farooq's public behavior disturbed many. His famous motorcycle-pillion ride with the prominent Indian actress Shabana Azmi to the Gulmarg meadow, a popular tourist attraction, became the grist of political columnists. It is small wonder that even while in office, he came to be known by the sobriquet "the disco chief minister."

One of the first challenges that Farooq faced after assuming office was the legacy of the Resettlement Bill. Though the state legislature had passed the bill, the governor, B. K. Nehru, had sent it back to the assembly, asking the legislature to amend the bill to deal with possible "unintended consequences."[56]

Prime Minister Indira Gandhi also entered the fray over this bill. In the election campaign leading up to the 1983 state assembly election, she and other Congress(I) leaders delivered speeches in

---

[55] For assessments of Sheikh Abdullah, see Nirmal Mukarji, "Sheikh Abdullah: Three Strands," *Mainstream*, September 18, 1982, 6–7, and Nikhil Chakravarty, "A Great Son of India," *Mainstream*, September 18, 1982, 25–26. Also see Balraj Puri, "The Era of Sheikh Mohammad Abdullah," *Economic and Political Weekly* 18:7 (February 1983): 233.

[56] Akbar, *Kashmir*, 198.

the predominantly Hindu area of Jammu and hinted that large numbers of Kashmiri Muslims would be able to enter the state from Pakistan. These fears were greatly exaggerated, but they fed the misgivings of Hindu voters in Jammu, who in any case had had an uneasy relationship with the National Conference, particularly in recent years.[57]

Farooq, though a political neophyte, had sufficient common sense to realize that attempts to alter this piece of legislation were politically unwise. He passed the bill through the state legislature by a voice vote on October 4, 1982. The president of India, Zail Singh, was opposed to the bill, under the advice of Indira Gandhi; nevertheless, he had little recourse but to send it off to the Supreme Court to assess its constitutional validity.

THE 1983 ELECTIONS

Farooq had displayed some sagacity in dealing with Indira Gandhi over the Resettlement Bill. However, he lacked the requisite political dexterity and skill to outwit Gandhi's concerted efforts to obtain a foothold for the Congress(I) in Jammu and Kashmir. As the state assembly elections of 1983 approached, Indira Gandhi dispatched her son, Rajiv Gandhi, as an emissary to Farooq Abdullah. Ostensibly she was interested in forging an electoral coalition with the National Conference. In reality she was interested in "seat adjustments"—a term that refers to an electoral agreement under which parties agree not to compete with each other in particular constituencies.

Accordingly, Rajiv went to the Kashmir House on Prithviraj Road in New Delhi to meet with Farooq. Farooq, unwilling to confront a member of the Gandhi family directly, simply failed to show up. Farooq's response infuriated Indira Gandhi; she construed his absence as a calculated snub.

[57] Farooq Abdullah, *My Dismissal* (New Delhi: Vikas, 1985), 24. For Jammu's uneasy relationship with the National Conference, see Balraj Puri, *Simmering Volcano: Study of Jammu's Relations with Kashmir* (New Delhi: Sterling, 1983).

Farooq also associated with the various opposition parties at the national level. Specifically, he attended a conference held at Vijaywada in the southern state of Andhra Pradesh and organized by N. T. Rama Rao, an actor-turned-politician. Farooq's flirtation with national politics in concert with the opposition was particularly distressing to Indira Gandhi. No doubt she feared that if Abdullah successfully entered the national political mainstream, he might wean a portion of the Muslim vote away from the Congress(I). Furthermore, if he successfully emerged as a national figure, he would be able to bolster his own position in Jammu and Kashmir.

Within Kashmir, too, Farooq took steps to strengthen his political and organizational positions. As early as late November 1982 he had announced his intention to ban communal and secessionist organizations within the state. On January 22, 1983, his government published an ordinance that empowered it to enforce such a ban.[58]

At an organizational level, he secured the election of Sheikh Nazir Ahmed, an adopted son of Sheikh Abdullah, to the position of general secretary of the National Conference. Furthermore, he forged another electoral alliance with Mirwaiz Mohammed Farooq. Mirwaiz Farooq was one of the most prominent religious leaders in Kashmir, the nephew of the late Mirwaiz Yusuf Shah and the former head of the All Jammu and Kashmir Muslim Conference.[59] (This alliance was popularly referred to as the Sher-Bakra [lion-goat] alliance. The supporters of the sheikh were the *shers* and those of the Mirwaiz, the *bakras*.)[60] In the process, he

---

[58] All-India Radio, Delhi Domestic Service, January 22, 1983, as reported in FBIS-NES, January 24, 1983.

[59] There is more than a modicum of irony to the forging of this accord. In the 1930s and 1940s, Sheikh Abdullah and Yusuf Shah were sworn enemies. See Inderjit Badhwar, "Kashmir Coalition: Will It Work?" *India Today*, November 30, 1986, 10–20, and Roop Krishen Bhatt, "Kashmir: The Politics of Integration," in *State Politics in India*, ed. Iqbal Narain (New Delhi: Meenakshi Prakashan, 1976), 148.

[60] P. S. Verma, *Jammu and Kashmir at the Political Crossroads* (New Delhi: Vikas, 1994), 148.

managed to fend off the challenge posed by his brother-in-law G. M. Shah.

On June 5, 1983, elections were held for the Jammu and Kashmir state assembly. This was the first election held in the state since the death of Sheikh Mohammed Abdullah. The election was essentially a two-way contest between the Congress(I) and the National Conference. In the election campaign, the National Conference had stressed that the central government of Indira Gandhi was intent on reducing the autonomy of the state. The Congress(I), for its part, dwelled on the issues of alleged corruption and economic mismanagement. Additionally, Indira Gandhi allegedly made veiled sectarian appeals in the campaign in Jammu.[61]

Despite Mrs. Gandhi's active campaigning on behalf of the Congress(I), the National Conference won handily. Although Farooq was a far cry from his towering father, considerable support still existed in Kashmir for the Abdullah family. The National Conference won forty-six seats, the Congress(I) twenty-six, and various other parties three seats. One seat in the Doda constituency was annulled by the Election Commission on grounds of electoral fraud. The Congress(I) candidate in the valley, Mufti Mohammed Sayeed, lost both the seats he had contested.

Largely based on its performance in Jammu, where Indira Gandhi had allegedly played the "Hindu card," the Congress(I) emerged as the principal opposition party in the state.[62] For the

---

[61] Ibid., 149. See also Inder Malhotra, *Indira Gandhi: A Personal and Political Biography* (London: Hodder and Stoughton, 1989), 277–9. Officials of considerable personal integrity who accompanied Mrs. Gandhi on the campaign trail provide a very different picture, however. They concede that she did campaign vigorously against the Resettlement Bill. However, they insist that there was no communal tenor to her remarks. On the other hand, they suggest that there may have been an element of personal pique against Abdullah. (Author interview with senior Indian government official, New York, March 1995.)

[62] Author interview with Amitabh Mattoo, then assistant editor of the *Independent* (New Delhi), January 31, 1994. In Jammu, according to Mattoo, Indira Gandhi successfully polarized the two communities. One of her principal campaign themes was the danger that the Resettlement Bill posed of a Muslim deluge into the state.

most part, polling was peaceful, but there were some cases of
electoral violence. The most significant incidence occurred after
the election in Srinagar on June 14, where rioting took the life of
one person and left several hundred people injured.[63] Although
there was disaffection with the central government in New Delhi
in this election, there was little public display of secessionist sentiment.[64] Kashmiris, particularly in the valley, still clung to the
National Conference and the legacy of Sheikh Abdullah.

CENTER-STATE TENSIONS

The outcome of this election was unacceptable to Indira Gandhi.
Certain propensities that had long characterized her style of governance had come to the fore in the early 1980s. These included
her unwillingness to allow the emergence of any new indigenous
political forces or organizations throughout the nation. Simultaneously, she evinced a strong proclivity to centralize power in New
Delhi. Paul Brass has commented quite cogently on these dual
tendencies:

> The centralizing and nationalizing measures taken by Mrs. Gandhi
> included: the political destruction of the state political bosses; the
> selection of the chief ministers of the Congress-dominated states by
> Mrs. Gandhi herself in consultation with her small clique of advis-
> ers; the increased use of President's Rule in the states; the increased
> use of central police and intelligence forces to monitor and control
> regional opposition; populist, demagogic appeals to national cate-
> gories of voters, such as the poor, the landless, and the minorities;
> and some manipulation of xenophobic and paranoiac nationalism
> against Pakistan and the American CIA.[65]

This strategy frequently resulted in self-fulfilling prophecies.
The central government under Indira Gandhi insisted on charac-
terizing every demand for local autonomy as potentially secession-

---

[63] *Keesing's Contemporary Archives* 29 (1983): 32438.
[64] Author interview with Anupam Dhar, an official government of India
election observer, New Delhi, January 2, 1994.
[65] Brass, *Politics of India,* 321–2.

ist and virtually every indigenous leader as treasonous. In response, the prime minister frequently resorted to a variety of dubious measures, including the dismissal of legitimately elected governments. With political activity effectively undermined, the disaffection within various states simply took on more radical hues.[66] As these movements turned violent and occasionally secessionist, Mrs. Gandhi had to use the full panoply of coercive power at the disposal of the Indian state. In the process she systematically corroded the quality of India's political life. Well-established norms were weakened, institutional procedures subverted, and corrupt and venal methods of governance increasingly rendered acceptable.

This all-too-familiar pattern also manifested itself in her dealings with Farooq Abdullah during 1983–4. Indira Gandhi had already taken exception to Abdullah's unwillingness to enter into an electoral alliance with the Congress(I) in contesting the 1983 election. Her misgivings were strengthened when Abdullah participated in a series of four opposition conclaves held in Vijaywada, New Delhi, Srinagar, and Calcutta during 1983–4.

At the Srinagar meeting, which was held October 5–8, 1983, Farooq took a leading role in criticizing the central government's propensity to arbitrarily dismiss legitimately elected state governments.[67] Unfortunately for Farooq, a group within the National Conference led by G. M. Shah, his brother-in-law, chose to publicly dissent from the party's position on center-state relations.[68] This dissidence within the ranks of the National Conference enabled the Congress(I) to undermine Farooq's hold on the party. The presence of Shah as a contender for the chief ministership of the state made the task easier. For his part, Shah had a small but sizable following in the assembly who would do his bidding.

[66] See, for example, "Muslim Fundamentalists Reemerging in Kashmir," *Statesman*, October 3, 1982, 9.
[67] All-India Radio, Delhi Domestic Service, October 8, 1983, as reported in FBIS-NES, October 11, 1983.
[68] All-India Radio, Delhi Domestic Service, October 4, 1983, as reported in FBIS-NES, October 4, 1983.

Some political analysts assert that a group of Indira Gandhi's advisers, led by Arun Nehru, Arif Mohammed Khan, and Mufti Mohammed Sayeed, urged her to oust Farooq. Sayeed, the head of the Congress(I) in Jammu and Kashmir, had a strong desire to be the next chief minister of Kashmir.[69] Unfortunately, these Congress(I) stalwarts and Indira Gandhi faced an important impediment in her efforts to remove Farooq Abdullah from office through dubious means. This roadblock lay in the form of her cousin Braj Kumar Nehru, the governor of Jammu and Kashmir. A senior member of the elite Indian Civil Service (ICS), Nehru had a reputation for probity and integrity. When Indira Gandhi suggested that Farooq Abdullah's regime be dismissed on rather tenuous grounds, Nehru firmly rebuffed her. Realizing that Nehru would not be any more tractable in the future, she removed him from the governorship of Jammu and Kashmir. In his place, on April 26, 1984, she appointed Jagmohan Malhotra, a former lieutenant-governor of New Delhi. Jagmohan had a reputation as an efficient if ruthless administrator. One of the more unsavory features of his professional life was his involvement in the harsh slum-clearance projects in New Delhi during Indira Gandhi's 1976–7 State of Emergency.[70]

THE DISMISSAL OF FAROOQ ABDULLAH

With the connivance of G. M. Shah and a faction of National Conference Members of the Legislative Assembly (MLAs) who were loyal to him, Jagmohan arranged for the dismissal of Farooq Abdullah's regime. After the legislators loyal to Shah professed that they no longer supported Farooq Abdullah, the National Conference lacked a majority in the state assembly. Within hours, on July 2, 1984, Jagmohan swore in G. M. Shah as the new chief minister.

It is not necessary to have a brief for Farooq Abdullah to argue that his dismissal was unwarranted and extraconstitutional. Few political commentators would contend that he was an especially

[69] Author interview with Kashmiri scholar, New Delhi, June 3, 1993.
[70] Bhattacharjea, *Kashmir*, 237.

able or skillful chief minister. Nevertheless, the reasons that were adduced for his dismissal were, at best, flimsy and, at worst, downright specious.[71] The ostensible charges and apparent evidence are as follows. First, he had both consorted with and consequently encouraged secessionist forces within the state. One of the accusations leveled against him was that he had sought the support of Mirwaiz Mohammed Farooq, the mirwaiz of Kashmir, in the 1983 election. The mirwaiz, an important religious figure, had, on occasion, criticized the central government and had also urged his followers to boycott the election.

There is little question that Farooq Abdullah had sought the mirwaiz's support.[72] However, that in itself can hardly be deemed treasonous. If anything, Abdullah's overtures toward the mirwaiz probably helped bring him into the political mainstream.

Second, it was alleged that Farooq had permitted Sikh terrorists to train in Kashmir and that he had met with Sant Jarnail Singh Bhindranwale, the charismatic and violent Sikh preacher who had taken refuge in the Golden Temple in Amritsar. Both these charges are apparently correct. It is a fact that some Sikh *gurmat* (religious training) camps were held in Jammu and Kashmir. Given the widespread disturbances in the Punjab in the early 1980s, Farooq's tolerance of such activity without careful scrutiny shows a degree of inattention to politically sensitive issues. Such neglect, however, hardly constituted adequate grounds for the dismissal of his regime. If such a rigorous standard were to be followed, Indira Gandhi should also have dismissed other state governments. Most notably, the Marxist regime of Jyoti Basu in West Bengal would have been a prime candidate for dismissal. After all, it had failed to prevent Sikh extremists from obtaining medical treatment in Calcutta throughout much of the 1980s.[73]

---

[71] Jagmohan Malhotra spells out the charges against Abdullah in his self-aggrandizing work. See Jagmohan, *My Frozen Turbulence in Kashmir* (New Delhi: Allied, 1991).

[72] Abdullah admits as much. See Abdullah, *My Dismissal*, 28.

[73] Author interview with senior journalist, *Times of India*, Calcutta, May 29, 1991.

Abdullah's much-made-of meeting with Bhindranwale also amounts to little. The meeting took place during a ceremonial visit that he had paid to the Golden Temple in Amritsar. It lasted all of fifteen minutes. The symbolism of the meeting, however, was infelicitous. At this time it was well known to all political observers in India that Bhindranwale had close links with various secessionist Sikh groups in the Punjab.

DRIFTING TOWARD INSURGENCY

The installation of the Shah regime following Farooq Abdullah's dismissal convinced the vast majority of Kashmiris in the valley that the national government had a reckless disregard for constitutional procedures. Shah's government was widely unpopular. If Farooq was known as the "disco chief minister," Shah quickly became known as the "curfew chief minister"; his propensity to impose curfews to maintain civil order in Srinagar and throughout much of the Kashmir valley was legendary.

The potential sources of instability within Kashmir were manifold. In part, Shah's regime faced significant opposition from the Farooq faction of the National Conference. As the ousted chief minister, Farooq did not have the temperament to quietly lick his political wounds. Instead he and his political supporters remained intent on harassing the Shah regime.

Shah's regime, in turn, appeared equally determined to tar and feather Farooq. Among other matters, a cabinet subcommittee of the Shah government released a report on January 9, 1985, which accused the previous regime of engaging in financial irregularities and of ignoring intelligence organizations' reports about the rise of secessionist sentiment and activity within the state.[74]

As the Shah government and Farooq Abdullah and his supporters traded charges, the security and economic situation in the state started to worsen. The poor economic conditions that spawned

[74] "Interim Report on Abdullah Government in Kashmir," All-India Radio, Delhi Domestic Service, January 9, 1985, as reported in FBIS-NES, January 10, 1985.

high unemployment among semi-educated youth provided a fertile recruiting ground for various secessionist organizations such as the Jammat-i-Islami, its Jammat-i-Tulba youth wing, and the People's League. These organizations started to extend their political sinews with increasing impunity. They successfully ensured the closure of bars in Srinagar and of liquor stores in the smaller towns of Anant nag and Sopore. More ominously, they pressured university authorities in Srinagar to ban the circulation of books that they deemed to be anti-Islamic.[75] These forms of illegal activity could continue within the state principally because the demands of political survival sapped the limited energies of the Shah regime. No orchestrated strategy was fashioned to deal with the increasing boldness of separatist organizations. Challenges from other, legitimate opposition parties, often in the form of strikes and demonstrations, added to the problems that the regime faced.[76]

The central government, now under the leadership of Rajiv Gandhi and flush after its major electoral victory, did little to prod the Shah regime to improve political effectiveness. It tended to view the internal politics of the state through the narrow prism of law, order, and security. Little effort was expended to examine and address the underlying sources of discontent within this politically sensitive state. Instead the central government continued to expand the stunning array of draconian legislation ostensibly designed to curb terrorist activity. In practice, legislation such as the Terrorist and Disruptive Activities Prevention Act (TADA) provided police and paramilitary forces with sweeping powers of arrest and detention. To provide the government of Jammu and Kashmir with the legal wherewithal to arrest and detain individuals suspected of having links with secessionist organizations, the central government extended the provisions of TADA to Kashmir

---

[75] It is also alleged that on occasion these groups received the tacit support of Farooq Abdullah for reasons of political expediency. "Pakistan Training Extremists," All-India Radio, Delhi Domestic Service, January 9, 1985, as reported in FBIS-NES, January 10, 1985.

[76] "Srinagar Strike 'Almost Total'; Minister Cited," All-India Radio, Delhi Domestic Service, May 6, 1985, as reported in FBIS-NES, May 7, 1985.

on June 5, 1985.[77] Later that summer, Parliament passed a bill that further extended the provisions of TADA in the state.

The state government undertook other security measures. In September the Jammu and Kashmir government declared some six hundred villages as a restricted area. All men over the age of eighteen were issued identity cards, and paramilitary patrols were stepped up in the region. The government justified this decision on the grounds that the area had become one of the principal avenues for Pakistani infiltration into the state.[78]

At best, these measures were ameliorative. They may have limited the activities of pro-Pakistani and secessionist organizations. At worst, they only added to the burdens of ordinary Kashmiris. The ability of the security forces to act with impunity under the aegis of TADA led to increasing high-handedness and contempt for the sentiments of the local population. In effect, the very measures that had been undertaken to curb violent secessionist activity fed the existing reservoir of discontent and resentment.

Finally, Abdullah's detractors alleged that he had been secretly in touch with the secessionist Plebiscite Front sympathizers during his years in London and in Pakistan-Occupied Kashmir (POK), or "Azad Kashmir" (literally, "Free Kashmir"). Again, this allegation has elements of truth. In 1974 Abdullah had met with members of this secessionist organization. Later they had invited him to the town of Mirpur in POK. Apparently, little of significance had transpired at Mirpur. Principally, the leaders of the Plebiscite Front had sought to convey their concerns about the ongoing dialogue between Sheikh Mohammed Abdullah and Indira Gandhi.[79] Although these contacts had taken place almost a decade before Farooq Abdullah's formal entry into political life, they became useful political fodder in the hands of his antagonists in 1984.

---

[77] "Anti-Terrorist Bill to Be Applicable in Kashmir," All-India Radio, Delhi Domestic Service, June 6, 1985, as reported in FBIS-NES, June 6, 1985.

[78] "Kashmir Declares 600 Villages Restricted Areas," All-India Radio, Delhi Domestic Service, September 15, 1985, as reported in FBIS-NES, September 16, 1985.

[79] Abdullah, *My Dismissal*, 30.

CONCLUSIONS

The government of India failed to translate the gains of the 1971 war into the permanent advantage of the Indian state, both at the level of foreign policy and at the level of domestic politics, as far as the Kashmir issue was concerned. Its main failure was not converting the LOC into an international border, a lapse that left Pakistan with the opportunity to revisit the issue at a later date.

More disturbing, the domestic gains of the 1971 war were also frittered away. The 1975 Beg-Parthasarathi Accord, despite all its limitations, could have placed the central government's relations with Kashmir on a more secure footing. Unfortunately, even the limited provisions of the accord were never implemented. Worse still, the central government, except during the Janata interregnum, contributed to the further decay of political institutions in the state.

In the background of this political scene, Kashmiris were becoming better educated and more politically aware. Younger Kashmiris, no longer as politically quiescent as their parents, began to chafe against the steady suppression of political dissent. Finding virtually all institutional channels of expressing their discontent closed, they mobilized and resorted to other, more violent methods of protest. Since secular politics, as represented by the National Conference, was corrupt and undemocratic, it is not surprising that the movement took on an ethnoreligious dimension.

It needs to be reiterated that only some of the precipitating conditions of the insurgency were present in earlier periods. Pakistan had tried and failed to foment an insurgency in 1964–5. In 1971, Kashmiris had ample opportunity to create havoc for India as it waged war with Pakistan. Yet in neither instance did the Kashmiris revolt. Only when a new generation came of political age under the sleight-of-hand of the national government did the population of the valley resort to a violent insurrection. The next chapter will bring us to this outbreak.

5

The proximate causes:
The Rajiv-Farooq Accord and
the outbreak of the insurgency

The two preceding chapters spelled out key components of the central argument of this book by studying specific eras in Kashmir's recent history: 1962 to 1965 and 1971 to 1986. Chapter 2 explained the rise of political mobilization in Kashmir and traced the accelerating process of political decay, two factors that combined to create the underlying conditions for the insurgency. This chapter will examine the proximate causes of the insurgency: the formation of an electoral alliance between the Congress(I) and Farooq Abdullah in November 1986 and the flawed election of 1987.

Forging an electoral alliance with the Congress(I), a mere two years after his crass dismissal reduced him to the status of a stalking-horse for the Congress(I) in Kashmir. It largely stripped Farooq of the political mantle he had inherited from his father. But the electoral skulduggery of 1987 was fraught with even greater political significance. It conveyed a message that the Kashmiris of the valley simply would not be allowed or trusted to freely exercise their franchise. In effect, the corruption of the electoral process in 1987 ensured that the last viable avenue for the expression of political discontent was blocked.

Farooq's dismissal in 1984 had demonstrated to a new generation of politically conscious Kashmiris the flagrant disregard that the regime in New Delhi had for constitutional norms and prerogatives. Previous generations had been far more willing to tolerate

New Delhi's political machinations. Those in the newly emergent generation proved to be considerably less passive. In addition to their political grievances, the paucity of adequate economic opportunities fueled their resentment against New Delhi. As one observer has remarked:

> A new generation of Kashmiris, who knew little or nothing of the freedom movement against the Maharaja's rule or the tribal invasion, had gone to the polls, and were disappointed. They had benefited from the free education—from primary to university levels—available since the early fifties, but were frustrated because there were few jobs available for them. Educated unemployed are the most eruptive element in any society; here, they blamed lack of opportunities in the rest of India for their plight.[1]

The other proximate causes of the insurgency can be located in events in Kashmir in the late 1980s. First, within India there was growing communal tension, resulting in repeated outbreaks of violence that had their repercussions in Kashmir.[2] Second, members of the Congress(I) regime in New Delhi desired to install a Congress(I) government in Jammu and Kashmir regardless of the potentially adverse consequences.

The Congress(I) regime did not have to wait long. Periodic rioting and bombings disrupted life in the valley. Indian intelligence agencies frequently reported on the growth of secessionist sentiment and fundamentalist fervor. The government of G. M. Shah proved to be singularly ineffectual in curbing protest activities.[3] Furthermore, its administrative capacities left much to be desired. It was markedly unresponsive when the Kashmir valley

---

[1] Ajit Bhattacharjea, *Kashmir: The Wounded Valley* (New Delhi: UBSPD, 1994), 253.

[2] This assertion leads to an important question: Why had Kashmir been isolated from the consequences of previous outbreaks of communal violence? The answer goes to the very heart of the argument of this book. Earlier generations of Kashmiris were not nearly as politically aware as those that emerged in the late 1970s and early 1980s. A far more politically sophisticated and better-informed Muslim populace was also more vocal about its corporate interests.

[3] Shekhar Gupta, "Extreme Claims," *India Today,* November 30, 1985, 22–3.

experienced unusually heavy snowfall in early January 1986. At one point, some 40 percent of Srinagar's six hundred thousand citizens went without water for five days.[4]

Further troubles befell the Shah regime in February 1986, when a judge vacated a long-standing court order that had sealed the Babri Mosque in the town of Ayodhya in Uttar Pradesh. The mosque, long the site of considerable political controversy, was believed to have been built by the Mughal emperor Babur after the demolition of a Hindu temple consecrating the birthplace of Lord Rama, a prominent member of the Hindu pantheon.[5] The opening of this long-disputed mosque to Hindu zealots disturbed the religious sentiments of significant sections of the Muslim community throughout India. In Kashmir, it served as a catalyst for communal violence. On February 15 in Srinagar, the local police opened fire on an unruly crowd that had gathered to protest the opening of the mosque. One protester was killed and several were injured.

Shortly thereafter, the Babri Mosque controversy and the police firing became embroiled with a local issue. The chief minister had made two rooms adjoining an old temple in the state offices in Jammu available to Muslim employees for worship. Some Hindu political activists in Jammu launched a protest against this decision, asserting that a mosque had been built next to the temple. Soon clashes broke out in Jammu between Hindu and Muslim activists. Before long the communal tensions had spread to other parts of the state, resulting in increased violence. Soon many towns in the Kashmir valley were placed under curfew. The task of maintaining law and order was increasingly turned over to the army and paramilitary forces as the local police proved to be either partisan or simply inadequately equipped to deal with the

[4] Ghulam Nabi Khayal, "Winter Blues," *India Today,* January 31, 1986, 18.
[5] Peter Van der Veer, "Ayodhya and Somnath: Eternal Shrines, Contested Histories," *Social Research* 59:1 (Spring 1992): 97. On December 6, 1992, a horde of Hindu zealots belonging to the Rashtriya Swyam Sevak Sangh and the Bajrang Dal, both affiliates of the Bharatiya Janata Party, attacked and demolished the Babri mosque. The demolition of the mosque sparked widespread rioting throughout much of India.

escalating violence.[6] The rising tide of violence against Hindus and the inability of the Shah regime to contain it, despite the frequent imposition of curfews, led to an exodus of the pandit population into Jammu. This initial migration prefigured a much larger move that would take place in 1990 as the spate of communal violence crested.

The governor of Jammu and Kashmir, Jagmohan Malhotra, who had played a critical role in Farooq Abdullah's dismissal, had little use for the Shah government.[7] On March 7, 1986, Jagmohan dismissed the Shah regime on the grounds of corruption and an inability to handle the growing political instability. Specifically, Jagmohan accused the Shah regime of the unconditional release of pro-Pakistani and secessionist elements, the attempted recruitment of "known communal elements" for the state administration and for two additional battalions of the Kashmir Armed Police (KAP), the sale of government leasehold land to occupants at half the market price, and the use of nepotism in filling state jobs.[8] Under the powers vested in him, Jagmohan declared President's Rule.

Jagmohan's stint as governor produced a mixed record. On the one hand he appeared to be an able administrator. Shortly after assuming office, he drew up plans for cleaning the Dal Lake in Srinagar, pushed through public housing construction projects, expanded the development of tourist resorts in Gulmarg and Pahalgam, and boosted the development of hydroelectric power.[9] On the other hand there are allegations that during his tenure in office, the recruitment of Muslims to higher administrative offices dropped noticeably.[10]

---

[6] P. S. Verma, *Jammu and Kashmir at the Political Crossroads* (New Delhi: Vikas, 1994), 215–7.

[7] Bhattacharjea, *Kashmir*, 248–50.

[8] Much of this evidence has been drawn from Philip E. Jones, "Paradise Lost: The Revolt in Kashmir" (South Asia Division, Office of Near East and South Asia Analysis, Central Intelligence Agency, Washington, D.C., 1990, photocopy), 17.

[9] Prabhu Chawla, "Cleaning Up," *India Today*, April 15, 1986, 32.

[10] Bhattacharjea, *Kashmir*, 251. Also see Jones, "Paradise Lost," 21.

THE RAJIV-FAROOQ ACCORD

On November 6, 1986, Prime Minister Rajiv Gandhi and Farooq Abdullah signed an accord that returned Farooq to the chief ministry of Jammu and Kashmir. One of the principal architects of this accord was Rajesh Pilot, the parliamentary minister in charge of surface transport. Pilot, who had gained the trust of Indira Gandhi, also proved to be a Rajiv Gandhi loyalist. He had displayed shrewd political instinct in carrying out previous party assignments. Accordingly, Rajiv Gandhi utilized him to serve as the party's emissary to Farooq and Jagmohan.[11]

What were Farooq's motivations for entering into this accord with Rajiv Gandhi? After all, this was the same government that had orchestrated his dismissal in 1984. Farooq no doubt realized that unless he made peace with the Congress(I) regime in New Delhi, there was little prospect of his returning to the chief ministry in the immediate future. Furthermore, he was led to believe that an alliance with the ruling party at the national level would bring substantial development funds to Jammu and Kashmir.[12] He is reported to have said: "In Kashmir, if I want to run a government, I have to stay on the right side of the Centre. That is the hard political reality I have come to accept."[13]

Despite the euphoria surrounding the accord, it reduced Abdullah's stature in Kashmir's internal politics. No longer was he seen as a Kashmiri standing up for the state's interests. Furthermore,

[11] Sreekant Khandekar, "Rajesh Pilot: The Trouble Shooter," *India Today,* November 30, 1986, 18. Rajiv had another reason to rely on Pilot. Rajiv's cousin Arun Nehru, the former minister of state for internal security, held long-standing grudges against Farooq. Nehru had wanted to install his protégé, the Union Minister of Tourism Mufti Mohammed Sayeed, as chief minister instead of Farooq. In the end, Arun Nehru lost his bid and was dismissed from his ministerial position. Conversations with senior officials in the prime minister's office indicate that Arun Nehru was dismissed from his position principally because of his intrigue that resulted in the opening of the Babri Mosque in Ayodhya.

[12] Verma, *Jammu and Kashmir,* 135.

[13] As quoted in Jones, "Paradise Lost," 23.

since the one secular party in the state had become the political ally of the Congress(I), the only other avenues of opposition, particularly in the Kashmir valley, were the religiously oriented and fundamentalist political parties, such as the Jammat-i-Islami, the Ummat-e-Islam, and the Mahaz-i-Azadi. Before long these parties would join to form the Muslim United Front (MUF) to contest the fateful 1987 elections.

The Congress(I), in turn, also damaged its standing in Jammu. Previously its popularity in Jammu had depended, at least in part, on its putative ability to defend the region from so-called Kashmiri (i.e., Kashmiri Muslim) domination. Having forged an alliance with the National Conference, it could no longer fulfill such a role.[14]

As the state assembly elections of June 1987 approached, Farooq campaigned relentlessly. He traversed the valley with his simple campaign message: The accord with the central government would ensure that Kashmir would receive its fair share of development funds. On the campaign trail, all appeared well—large crowds came out to greet him warmly. Nevertheless, an undercurrent of tension was already noticeable. Large crowds also showed up for the MUF candidates.[15] MUF leaders such as Qazi Nissar and Ali Shah Geelani routinely denounced the Rajiv-Farooq Accord and attacked Farooq's message of secularism. The crowds responded enthusiastically.[16]

---

[14] Balraj Puri, "Rajiv-Farooq Accord: What Went Wrong?" *Economic and Political Weekly* 24:30 (July 29, 1989): 1689–90.

[15] The MUF had been formed on September 2, 1986, in response to a number of developments within Jammu and Kashmir and elsewhere in the nation, including anger against the Rajiv-Farooq Accord, increasing communal violence within Jammu and Kashmir, and the emergence of fundamentalist sentiment in the Muslim world. The principal components of the MUF were the Jammat-i-Islami, the Ummat-e-Islam, Anjumane Ittehad-ul-Musalmeen, the Islamic Study Circle, the Muslim Education Trust, the Muslim Welfare Society, Islamic Jammat-i-Tulba, Majlis Tahafazul ul-Islami, Mahaz-i-Azadi, Jamiat-ul-Hadis, Shia Rabita Committee, and Idara Tahquiqat Islami. See Verma, *Jammu and Kashmir,* 76.

[16] Inderjit Badhwar, "Testing the Accord," *India Today,* March 31, 1987, 22–6.

THE ELECTION AND ITS AFTERMATH

The state assembly elections were held in April 1987. Every dispassionate account of the electoral proceedings points to blatant malfeasances on the part of the Congress(I)–National Conference alliance workers. Voters were systematically intimidated, ballot boxes were tampered with, and electoral officers were harassed by party workers. Furthermore, two weeks before the election, some six hundred opposition workers were arrested in those areas known to be MUF strongholds.[17]

The results of this flawed election were entirely predictable. The Congress(I)–National Conference alliance won sixty out of seventy-six seats. (The Congress(I) won twenty-four and the National Conference, thirty-six.) It is interesting to note that even though the alliance obtained a two-thirds majority, it polled just under 50 percent of the popular vote. Furthermore, even in Farooq's own constituency, Ganderbal, the percentage of votes cast for him declined by as much as 20 percent. An MUF candidate contesting Farooq on his home ground managed to capture 18 percent of the vote.[18]

The conduct and outcome of this election effectively closed the last possible venue for the expression of legitimate dissent in

[17] Author interviews with senior Indian government officials, New Delhi, June 1991, and author interviews with several journalists in New Delhi, January 1995. Also see Inderjit Badhwar, "A Tarnished Triumph," *India Today*, April 15, 1987, 40–42. According to a senior officer in the Indian Administrative Service (IAS) who was posted in Srinagar, ten seats in particular were compromised. In his view the electoral malfeasance profoundly contributed to the reservoir of anger and bitterness against the government of India among younger Kashmiris. Three individuals—Hamid Sheikh, Ashfaq Majid Wani, and Yasin Malik—were electoral workers during the 1987 elections. Later they all became important figures in the insurgency.

[18] Badhwar, "A Tarnished Triumph," 41. According to a senior IAS official who had known sympathies for the Kashmiris and who was closely connected with the electoral process, the manipulation of the electoral process is indisputable. In his assessment, some ten seats were affected. He does concede that the electoral malfeasances powerfully contributed to the sense of disillusionment among Kashmiri youths. (Author interview with senior IAS officer, September 1995.)

Kashmir. Abdul Ghani Lone, a former leader of the opposition and an MUF candidate, best expressed the sense of frustration of many Kashmiris: "This simply deepens people's feelings against the Government of India. If people are not allowed to cast their votes where will their venom go except into expressions of anti-national feelings?"[19]

Predictably, Farooq's troubles were not long in coming. By the fall of 1987 he had to start relying on protection by a retinue of police and paramilitary escorts to ensure his safety. Large numbers of police had to be deployed even when he went to offer prayers during the festival of Id-ul-Zuha in Srinagar. Resentment against his regime continued to mount as he proved incapable of tackling Kashmir's chronic problems of unemployment and poor infrastructure.

Of course, Farooq was not the only one to blame. The Congress(I) government in New Delhi was preoccupied with its own problems and paid little attention to Jammu and Kashmir. At a domestic level, the regime faced an increasingly hostile opposition, which accused the ruling party of having received substantial kickbacks for the purchase of the Bofors field gun for the Indian army. The party's electoral base had also shrunk considerably, with the Congress(I) in power in only twelve states. At the foreign policy level, in January 1987 India and Pakistan had teetered on the brink of war. "Brasstacks," India's largest military exercise in its postindependence history and a brainchild of General Krishnaswami Sundarji, had precipitated this crisis.[20] Furthermore, several divisions of the Indian army that had been deployed in Sri Lanka as the Indian Peace Keeping Force (IPKF) became steadily embroiled in the civil war there.[21] Though the IPKF was originally

---

[19] Abdul Ghani Lone, as quoted in Badhwar, "A Tarnished Triumph," 41.

[20] For a detailed description and analysis of "Exercise Brasstacks," see Kanti Bajpai, P. R. Chari, Pervaiz Iqbal Cheema, Stephen P. Cohen, and Šumit Ganguly, *Brasstacks and Beyond: Perception and the Management of Crisis in South Asia* (New Delhi: Manohar, 1995).

[21] For a thoughtful discussion of the Indian involvement in Sri Lanka, see S. D. Muni, *The Pangs of Proximity* (New Delhi: Sage, 1994).

intended to serve as a neutral force between the Liberation Tigers of Tamil Eelam (LTTE) and the Sri Lankan armed forces, its role was quickly transformed. By December 1987 it was conducting "Operation Pawan," designed to disarm the recalcitrant LTTE guerrillas.

The Congress(I) regime's distraction and Farooq's inability to govern certainly strengthened the influence of the MUF and also persuaded Mufti Mohammed Sayeed, who had resigned from Rajiv Gandhi's cabinet as minister for tourism, to throw down the gauntlet in Kashmir. Ostensibly, Sayeed resigned in August 1987 generally over the issue of communalism and specifically over the government's weak response to anti-Muslim riots in the city of Meerut in Uttar Pradesh. It also stands to reason that he harbored a grievance against Rajiv Gandhi over the latter's treatment of him during the negotiations leading to the Rajiv-Farooq Accord. Mufti Sayeed returned to the valley, where large crowds greeted him enthusiastically.[22]

THE GOVERNMENTAL MOVE AGITATION

As 1987 drew to a close, Farooq's difficulties mounted. Owing to the peculiar geography of Jammu and Kashmir, the state's administrative offices had moved to Jammu from Srinagar during the winter months. This practice dated back to 1870 to the reign of Maharaja Ranbir Singh. In modern times the size of the state government had expanded significantly, numbering thirty-seven departments with over five thousand employees. Consequently, the annual move had become a logistical and fiscal burden on the state. The Justice Gajendragadkar Commission, which had been appointed to examine the question of regional imbalances among Jammu, the Kashmir valley, and Ladakh, had noted in 1967, without providing any recommendations, that this move was a drain on the exchequer. Since then many discussions had been

---

[22] Inderjit Badhwar, "Farooq under Fire," *India Today,* September 15, 1987, 22–7. Other observers question the degree of enthusiasm with which he was greeted.

held in the state legislature about altering the terms of the annual move. However, on every occasion, the divergent pulls from Jammu and Srinagar brought most discussions to a quick halt. Legislators from Jammu had long claimed that their section of the state was neglected, while legislators from the Kashmir valley resented the demands of Jammu.[23]

Apart from the merits of these arguments, there were sound administrative reasons for putting an end to the annual move.[24] Unfortunately, the manner in which Farooq Abdullah decided to alter the existing arrangements angered many of the political notables in Jammu. Quite abruptly on October 7, 1987, without adequate prior public consultation and debate, Farooq Abdullah announced his government's intention to retain some twenty departments in Srinagar year-round. Among these offices were the Industries Department and the Financial Commissionerate. Farooq's announcement was greeted with considerable anger in Jammu. The Jammu Bar Association, in particular, vigorously criticized the decision and started public demonstrations against the move. Communal parties and organizations like the Bharatiya Janata Party (BJP) and the Shiv Sena also entered the fray, insisting that Abdullah's decision was prejudicial to the interests of the residents of Jammu. Faced with increasing public disturbances, coupled with pressure from the central government, particularly in the form of a highly publicized visit of Minister for Home Affairs Buta Singh, Farooq decided to rescind the order.

[23] Inderjit Badhwar, "End of the Honeymoon," *India Today*, December 15, 1987, 32–4.

[24] Farooq's decision had been prompted in part by a speech that Rajiv Gandhi gave in Srinagar in the winter of 1986. In this speech Rajiv had suggested that the Kashmir government might be more responsive to the needs of the population if it spent the summer months in Jammu and the winter months in Srinagar. (Author interview with senior Indian government official, August 1995.) In fairness, it needs to be mentioned that the cancellation of the annual move would inevitably inconvenience some. Thousands of *dhaba wallahs* (owners of small tea and food stalls), porters, and roadside hotel owners would be adversely affected if the move ended. (Personal communication with Professor Amitabh Mattoo, Jawaharlal Nehru University, March 25, 1996.)

His decision to backtrack from his initial position set off another series of disturbances, this time in the Kashmir valley. On this occasion the Bar Association of Srinagar spearheaded the agitation. As in Jammu, the issue quickly acquired communal overtones as the MUF declared that the chief minister was undermining the interests of Kashmiris. Accordingly, the MUF declared a general strike to press for the ouster of the coalition government. The leaders of the agitation now demanded that Srinagar be made the permanent capital of the state. By the end of November, the agitation largely petered out. However, the move issue had further delegitimized the Farooq regime.

1988: THE YEAR OF LIVING DANGEROUSLY

The year 1988 was a pivotal one for Farooq Abdullah's government. The preceding year had been marked by sporadic bursts of violence, riots, and strikes. However, a fundamentally qualitative change in the scope and extent of violence occurred during 1988. The violence went from being spasmodic to being orchestrated and deliberate. The targets of violence were carefully chosen, and the objectives of the perpetrators well exceeded the limited goal of removing the Congress(I)–Farooq Abdullah regime. The Kashmir insurgency, in an incipient form, had begun. Violence and instability in the valley became endemic in 1988.

The slightest pretext provided the basis for further agitation. In June, violence racked much of Srinagar when Farooq Abdullah's regime raised the electricity tariffs. Even though Farooq went out of his way to explain that 93 percent of the population would be unaffected by the tariff hikes, the violence continued unabated.[25]

The events that occurred in the wake of the abrupt death of General Zia-ul-Haq, the Pakistani military dictator, on August 17 revealed the depth of disaffection that was growing in the valley. Pro-Pakistani demonstrators surged through the streets of Srina-

[25] All-India Radio, Delhi Domestic Service, June 11, 1988, as reported in Foreign Broadcast Information Service, Near East and South Asia (FBIS-NES), June 14, 1988.

gar, defying a curfew and allegedly attacking Hindu homes; the police opened fire on them. The deaths of two demonstrators further inflamed passions, leading to more disturbances.

These demonstrations had barely subsided when another spate of violence swept through the valley. In late August, at the time of the festival of Muharrum, which condoles the death of the Prophet Mohammed's grandson Imam Husain, Shia-Sunni violence culminated in widespread arson and looting. The disturbances left one person dead and several hundred injured.

Both the Farooq Abdullah regime and the central government in New Delhi insisted that the rising tide of violence in Kashmir was Pakistani-sponsored.[26]

1989: KASHMIR ON THE EDGE

Violence continued to punctuate life in the valley as the new year started. As bombings, strikes, and demonstrations became virtually endemic, the government in New Delhi increasingly accused Pakistan of fomenting trouble in the valley. The Pakistani regime of Prime Minister Benazir Bhutto routinely denied the charges. At one point, in a seeming throwback to the days of Indira Gandhi, Home Affairs Minister Buta Singh even accused the U.S. Central Intelligence Agency (CIA) of supporting the Jammu and Kashmir Liberation Front (JKLF).[27] Buta Singh's fulminations against foreign instigation notwithstanding, thoughtful observers in India more accurately identified the sources of instability: The enemy lay within.[28]

The Farooq Abdullah regime seemed to share Buta Singh's assessment, however. In an act of desperation in late August, it passed legislation designed to prevent newspapers from printing

---

[26] All-India Radio, Delhi Domestic Service, October 15, 1988, as reported in FBIS-NES, October 17, 1988.

[27] "Pakistan, CIA Blamed for Kashmir Violence," *Indian Express,* June 23, 1989, 1.

[28] See, for example, the editorial "On the Brink," *Indian Express,* July 21, 1989, 8.

material that the government deemed prejudicial to public order. Understandably, a public outcry followed the passage of this bill. Even normally progovernment newspapers reacted sharply, denouncing the bill as an act of blatant censorship. One newspaper referred to the bill as "hare-brained."[29]

THE RUBAIYA SAYEED AFFAIR

Farooq's days in office were numbered. The Congress(I) government in New Delhi was defeated in the national elections of December 1989. A new, minority government emerged in New Delhi, with Vishwanath Pratap Singh, a former finance and defense minister, as prime minister. The new government had barely been sworn in when it faced its first crisis in Kashmir.

On December 8, JKLF activists abducted Rubaiya Sayeed, the daughter of the new minister for home affairs, Mufti Mohammed Sayeed. The event paralyzed the government in Jammu and Kashmir. In part, the government machinery stalled because Farooq Abdullah was abroad for medical treatment. The national government caved in to the demands of the kidnappers, exchanging Sayeed for five militants who had been incarcerated on various charges.[30] There is little question that the new government's willingness to promptly meet the demands of the abductors sent out an important signal. Insurgent groups throughout the valley saw that the government lacked the necessary discipline to stand firm when confronted by an act of terror.

The government of V. P. Singh not only acceded to the demands of the JKLF but also, and more important, failed to fashion a coherent strategy to deal with the emerging political crisis in Kashmir. In part, its inability to develop a programmatic response to the situation in Kashmir stemmed from its own internal weaknesses. The minority National Front government remained preoc-

[29] Agence France Presse Hong Kong, August 24, 1989, as reported in FBIS-NES-89-164, August 25, 1989.

[30] Pankaj Pachauri, "Abduction Anguish," *India Today,* December 31, 1989, 38–41.

cupied with the imperatives of political survival in New Delhi. At the state level, Farooq Abdullah appeared at a complete loss to curb the growing lawlessness and violence. In crude attempts to restore order, Farooq increasingly relied on the police and paramilitary forces. His coalition government, which lacked legitimacy, could think of little else to do.[31] These harsh tactics served only to further alienate an already disenchanted population.

JAGMOHAN RETURNS

In January 1990, Farooq Abdullah resigned after Jagmohan Malhotra was reappointed the governor of the state, replacing the former chief of staff of the Indian army, General K. V. Krishna Rao, who had been serving as governor.[32] It is believed that V. P. Singh's principal advisers on Kashmir, Arun Nehru and Mufti Mohammed Sayeed, were instrumental in placing Jagmohan in the governorship. Both men reputedly believed that a degree of firmness was necessary in dealing with the Kashmiri insurgents. Other members of the Singh cabinet apparently shared this view.[33] In fairness to V. P. Singh's regime, it should be mentioned that in early March the regime granted independent charge over Kashmir to George Fernandes, the minister of state for railways. To assist Fernandes, it also constituted an advisory committee: Surendra Mohan, of the National Front; Ghulam Rasool Kar, of the Congress(I); Kedarnath Sahni, of the BJP; Saifuddin Chaudhury, of the Communist Party (Marxist); M. Farooqi, of the Communist Party; and P. L. Handoo, of the National Conference.[34] Fernandes, a

---

[31] Pankaj Pachauri and Zafar Meraj, "Drifting Dangerously," *India Today,* January 15, 1990, 4–7.

[32] For a discussion of the political intrigue surrounding the appointment of Jagmohan as governor, see George Fernandes, "The Way Out," *Seminar,* April 1992, 24–31.

[33] Tavleen Singh, *Kashmir: A Tragedy of Errors* (New Delhi: Viking/Penguin, 1995), 131.

[34] All-India Radio, Delhi Domestic Service, "Railway Minister to Look After Kashmir Affairs," March 13, 1990, as reported in FBIS-NES-90-049, March 14, 1990.

socialist trade union leader of long standing, sought to mitigate some of the harshness of Jagmohan's policies. However, he frequently found himself at odds with Home Affairs Minister Mufti Mohammed Sayeed.

Jagmohan's second tenure as governor started on a poor note. While he was at his swearing-in ceremony in Jammu, paramilitary troops opened fire against an unarmed crowd that had gathered at the Gawakadal bridge to protest a particularly harsh cordon-and-search operation earlier that day.[35] Jagmohan's approach to the insurgency in Kashmir echoed this opening omen—it was essentially repressive. He was also openly critical of Farooq Abdullah's administration, asserting that it had been corrupt and inefficient and had squandered state funds.[36]

In an unrelated development, which nevertheless inflamed public opinion in both India and Pakistan, Indian troops shot and killed three protesters, believed to be JKLF sympathizers, who attempted to cross the Line of Control (LOC) at a place called Chakothi in Pakistani Kashmir. The protesters had gathered there to mark the anniversary of the death of a JKLF leader, Maqbool Butt, who had been sent to the gallows for his part in the murder of a judge.[37]

Jagmohan's iron-handed strategy proved to be costly from the outset but had only very limited success in blunting the insurgency. Certainly, it did little to reduce the level of violence in the state. One of the first victims of the disturbed conditions in the state was its fabled tourist industry. Earlier in 1989 in a display of religious zealotry, militant Muslim insurgents, the Allah Tigers in particular, had shut down bars, video parlors, and movie theaters on the grounds that they were "un-Islamic." With the violence spiraling out of control, tourism, one of the principal sources of employ-

---

[35] Singh, *Kashmir: A Tragedy of Errors*, 132.

[36] Sanjoy Hazarika, "India Paves Way for Kashmir Elections," *New York Times*, February 20, 1990, A3.

[37] "Indian Troops Kill Three at Kashmir Cease-Fire Line," *New York Times*, February 12, 1990, A9.

ment in the state, sharply tapered off. The hardships that the decline in tourist traffic generated became yet another source of resentment against the government in New Delhi.[38]

Supporters of the government's "mailed fist" strategy claimed one of its more visible successes on March 30, when Ashfaq Majid Wani, one of the leaders of the JKLF, was killed in a clash with Indian security forces in Srinagar. The irony of this incident, however, was that Wani was killed when a grenade that he was carrying exploded in his hand.[39] Wani, one of the four principal leaders of the JKLF (along with Abdul Hamid Sheikh, Javed Mir, and Yasin Malik), had been implicated in the abduction of Rubaiya Sayeed.[40] As Jagmohan pursued his highly repressive strategy within Kashmir, the increasingly beleaguered Singh government in New Delhi sought to blame Pakistan for instigating and orchestrating the violence in Kashmir.[41]

As law and order in Kashmir deteriorated, relations between members of the minority pandit (Hindu) community and their Muslim counterparts in the valley started to fray. Historically, unlike other parts of India, Kashmir had not been witness to widespread communal tension and violence. However, two factors undermined the sense of security and safety of the pandit community in Kashmir. First, the governor hinted that the safety and security of the Hindu community could not be guaranteed. Second, the fanatical religious zeal of some of the insurgent groups instilled fear among the Hindus of the valley. By early March, according to one estimate, more than forty thousand

[38] Sanjoy Hazarika, "Political Strife Threatens Himalayas Tourism," *New York Times,* March 1, 1990, A11.

[39] Sanjoy Hazarika, "Liberation Leader and Ten Others Slain in Kashmir," *New York Times,* March 31, 1990.

[40] This group of four individuals—Abdul Hamid Sheikh, Ashfaq Majid Wani, Javed Mir, and Yasin Malik—was known by the acronym HAJY. (Author interview with Surjit Singh Oberoi, independent journalist, New Delhi, January 1995.)

[41] Barbara Crossette, "India's Growing Peril: Kashmir and Punjab Separatism," *New York Times,* April 17, 1990.

Hindu inhabitants of the valley had fled to the comparative safety of Jammu.[42]

This spiral of insurgent violence and the relentless pressure from Indian security forces continued through much of 1990. Two incidents deserve particular mention. The first, in early April, was the kidnapping and subsequent murder of three men: H. L. Khera, the manager of the state-run Hindustan Machine Tools factory in Srinagar; Mushirul Haq, the vice-chancellor of Kashmir University; and Haq's personal secretary, Abdul Ghani. The insurgents had offered to release all three individuals in exchange for a number of incarcerated insurgents. The government, which had previously given in to the demands of the kidnappers of Rubaiya Sayeed, refused to budge this time. Tragically, the government's gamble failed to pay off. Within the next few days, first Khera's and subsequently Haq's and Ghani's bullet-ridden bodies were found in different parts of Srinagar.

The other major incident involved both insurgent violence and state repression in its aftermath. Maulvi Mohammed Farooq, the mirwaiz of Kashmir and the leader of the Action Committee of the Kashmiri Awami movement, was killed in Srinagar on May 21. Reportedly, three men walked into the cleric's home and shot him in cold blood. Matters worsened considerably after the mirwaiz's death. During the funeral procession, as the mourners passed Islamia College, a trigger-prone paramilitary picket opened fire on the crowd, killing twenty people on the spot. Twenty-seven others later died of their wounds.[43]

This incident proved to be a significant setback for the Jagmo-

---

[42] Pratap Chakravarty, "Thousands of Hindus Flee Unrest in Kashmir," Agence France Presse Hong Kong, March 8, 1990, as reported in FBIS-NES-90-046, March 8, 1990.

[43] Ironically, the procession, when it first started out, had a strong anti–Hizb-ul-Mujahideen tone. (The Hizb-ul-Mujahideen was widely suspected of having killed the mirwaiz.) Once the shooting started, however, sentiment quickly shifted against the Indian government. (Personal communication with Professor Amitabh Mattoo, Jawaharlal Nehru University, March 25, 1996.)

han administration. His "mailed fist" tactics had done little to win the sympathies of the Kashmiris, even though hundreds of suspected insurgents had been arbitrarily arrested and incarcerated in sweeping cordon-and-search operations. Maulvi Farooq's murder, which propagandists for the various insurgent groups sought to pin on the Indian government's intelligence agents, further damaged the government's position.

6

The crisis worsens

As the violence in Kashmir continued to claim the lives of the insurgents, members of the security forces, and citizens, Indo-Pakistani relations worsened. Pakistani officials kept up a steady drumbeat of criticism of Indian actions in Kashmir. Pakistani Prime Minister Benazir Bhutto, who had initially sought to improve relations with India during the Rajiv Gandhi regime, increasingly found herself on the defensive as the opposition publicly assailed her for not taking a more unyielding position on Kashmir. In addition to stepping up her anti-Indian rhetoric, Bhutto dispatched her adviser on national security issues, Iqbal Akhund, in March to Washington, D.C., and Moscow to plead Pakistan's case.[1]

Indo-Pakistani relations reached what was probably their lowest ebb in May 1990. The precise details of the crisis that punctuated this worsening trend in Indo-Pakistani relations still remain murky, a subject of intense debate both on the subcontinent and in the United States.[2] According to one account, Indian leaders, increasingly frustrated by their inability to restore a degree of

---

[1] Madhu Jain, "Raising the Stakes," *India Today,* February 28, 1990, 19–21.

[2] Michael Krepon and Mishi Faruqee, eds., *Conflict Prevention and Confidence-Building Measures in South Asia: The 1990 Crisis,* Occasional Paper no. 17 (Washington, D.C.: Henry L. Stimson Center, 1994); Seymour Hersh, "On the Nuclear Edge," *New Yorker,* March 29, 1993.

order in Kashmir, had contemplated attacking insurgent sanctuaries and training bases in Pakistani Kashmir. To this end, it is argued, Indian troops were moved into Kashmir. Pakistani officials, on learning about Indian intentions through their intelligence services, placed the Pakistani Air Force on a nuclear alert.

American intelligence agencies picked up evidence of Indian troop movement and the corresponding Pakistani responses. Seeking to avoid what many in Washington, D.C., perceived to be a rapidly escalating trend in tensions, the U.S. deputy national security adviser, Robert Gates, and his assistant for the Near East and South Asia, Richard Haass, were sent to Islamabad and New Delhi to counsel restraint. In Islamabad, Gates informed the Pakistani leadership that in all the Pentagon's war-gaming scenarios involving an Indo-Pakistani conflict, Pakistan emerged as the clear loser. Consequently, Gates contended that it was in Pakistan's interest to rein in its support for the Kashmiri insurgents. In New Delhi, he counseled Indian decision-makers to exercise restraint in Kashmir and improve the human rights record of the security forces.[3] Some argue that Gates's counsel of restraint was heeded and that a potential conflict was thus avoided. Others contend that the crisis was effectively over before Gates reached the subcontinent.[4]

ENTER GIRISH SAXENA

In late May, Girish Chandra ("Gary") Saxena replaced Jagmohan Malhotra as the governor of Jammu and Kashmir. Saxena, a former head of the Research and Analysis Wing (RAW), India's premier counterintelligence agency, had considerable experience with counterinsurgency operations. The precise reasons for Jagmohan's departure are unclear. According to some accounts, he was

[3] John F. Burns, "U.S. Urges Pakistan to Settle Feud with India over Kashmir," *New York Times,* May 21, 1990.

[4] The most detailed and thoughtful analysis of the 1990 crisis can be found in Devin T. Hagerty, "The Theory and Practice of Nuclear Deterrence in South Asia" (Ph.D. diss., University of Pennsylvania, 1995). Also see Mitchell Reiss, *Bridled Ambition: Why Countries Constrain Their Nuclear Capabilities* (Washington, D.C.: Woodrow Wilson Center Press, 1995).

replaced because some members of V. P. Singh's government felt
that his harsh tactics had not yielded the requisite results. Furthermore, in the wake of the violence that had left more than one
hundred people dead after the assassination of Mirwaiz Mohammed Farooq, Jagmohan had become a political liability for the
government. The Congress(I), the largest opposition party in Parliament, and other parties had also become increasingly critical of
Jagmohan's performance as governor. Consequently, an individual
with greater finesse as well as counterinsurgency experience was
needed.

One of Saxena's first legal moves was the passage of the Jammu
and Kashmir Disturbed Areas Act on July 5. This act provided
sweeping powers to officers in the security forces. Specifically, it
authorized any magistrate or police officer of the rank of a subin-
spector or above to "use force even to the extent of causing death"
without permission from higher authorities. The passage of this
act gave the security forces the ability to act with impunity. In
turn, Indian and foreign civil liberties groups sharply criticized the
act on the same grounds.[5] Despite these harsh measures, the situation in Kashmir showed little or no improvement through much of
1990.

THE KUNAN-POSHPORA INCIDENT

It is certainly possible to contend that these unbridled powers of
the security forces contributed to a tragic incident near the village
of Kunan-Poshpora, located close to the Line of Control (LOC),
in late February 1991. Exactly what happened at this village after
a cordon-and-search operation on the night and early hours of the
morning of February 23–4 remains the subject of sharp disagree-
ment.[6]

---

[5] See, for example, Asia Watch and Physicians for Human Rights, *Kashmir: A Pattern of Impunity* (New York: Asia Watch, 1993).

[6] See, for example, Asia Watch, *Human Rights in India: Kashmir under Siege* (New York: Asia Watch, 1991), and Report of the Press Council of India, *Crisis and Credibility* (New Delhi: Lancer International, 1991).

Reading the various conflicting accounts of the events at the two villages is reminiscent of Akira Kurosawa's great film *Rashomon.*[7] Despite the differing versions of the incident, some basic facts about the Kunan-Poshpora incident can be assembled. On the night of February 23 and the early morning of February 24, the Fourth Rajputana Rifles Regiment of the Sixty-eighth Mountain Division entered the village of Kunan-Poshpora in the Kupwara district to conduct a cordon-and-search operation. Such operations, routinely undertaken in counterinsurgency procedures, involve a number of different steps. First, a specific geographical area is cordoned off and secured. Second, the inhabitants of the area are separated on the basis of age and gender. Third, a search party enters and systematically combs the houses for weaponry, logistical equipment, and other accoutrements belonging to the insurgents. Fourth, on the basis of prior information, selected inhabitants are questioned for their possible connections with the insurgents.

A cordon-and-search operation of the form described above did take place at Kunan-Poshpora. The contentious issues concern what may have occurred *after* the cordon-and-search operation. According to the accounts of human rights activists, no less than twenty-three and possibly as many as one hundred women were raped by the soldiers belonging to the Rajputana Rifles. Many of the soldiers, it is also alleged, were inebriated. Furthermore, the same accounts hold that the officers of the regiment were busy interrogating a number of the men of the village, leaving the soldiers to their own devices. At 9 A.M. on February 24, the army column withdrew from the villages, having obtained coerced "no-objection" forms signed by three village notables and two Jammu and Kashmir constables. Around March 3 or 4 the district magistrate of Kupwara, Syed Mohammed Yasin, having received reports of army misconduct, decided to investigate. With the two Jammu and Kashmir police constables who had accompanied the Rajpu-

---

[7] The film deals with the possible rape of a hapless woman by a passing bandit. The tale, narrated by seven individuals, provides seven differing versions of this supposedly tragic incident.

tana Rifles unit, he visited the villages around March 6. On reaching
the villages, he was informed of the tragedy that had occurred on
February 23–4. After his preliminary visit to the village, he contacted Wajahat Habibullah, the divisional commissioner of Jammu
and Kashmir. On March 18 Habibullah, accompanied by an army
intelligence officer, went to the village to conduct his own investigation. Habibullah found the allegations of mass rape less than con-
vincing. However, on the basis of his investigation, he concluded
that it was entirely possible that the soldiers may have used excessive force and may also have sexually harassed some of the women.

Accordingly, he drafted a report suggesting that a number of
precautions be taken to avoid a repetition of similar actions or
allegations of such. He also called for a further governmental
inquiry into the alleged incident. According to Habibullah, the
army accepted all his recommendations. The state government did
ask for an inquiry to be conducted; however, it was done in a
desultory manner, and the results were inconclusive.[8]

The official version, as may be expected, differs considerably. It
concedes that cordon-and-search operations are normally conducted during the day. This operation was conducted at night
because the villages were known as a staging ground for insurgents
and had previously been targeted by paramilitary forces. The operation started at about 11 P.M. on the night of February 23 with an
outer cordon being formed outside the village. The search started
around 1 A.M. the next morning, with two Jammu and Kashmir
police constables from the neighboring Trehgram Police Station
accompanying the Rajputana Rifles contingent. The search and
interrogation operations yielded little. Two AK-47s were found, as
well as one pistol with a limited cache of ammunition. After
completing a second search, the army unit left around 9 A.M.
Before leaving, the army medical personnel set up a mobile medical unit and treated twenty-three individuals, including eight
women who subsequently claimed that they were victims of the
mass rape. Later the same morning the brigadier commanding the

---

[8] Personal correspondence with Wajahat Habibullah, minister for community affairs, Embassy of India, Washington, D.C., November 1995.

Sixty-eighth Mountain Division visited the village and spoke to the headman and other notables. No complaints against the army's operation were submitted to him.

Faced with accusations from human rights organizations, the Indian army asked the Press Council of India to investigate the charges of mass rape. Accordingly, the Press Council empowered a well-known journalist, B. G. Verghese, to conduct an independent investigation, and the Press Council group visited Kunan-Poshpora on June 11, 1991. Clearing the army of any accusation of wrong-doing, the Press Council reported that the charges had been fabricated by villagers sympathetic to the militancy. The Press Council report, in turn, came under considerable criticism.[9]

What exactly happened at Kunan-Poshpora? The true story may never be unraveled. The villagers' accounts cannot be accepted as completely reliable because they are riddled with inconsistencies. The Press Council report appears too ready to grant the army the benefit of the doubt. As Wajahat Habibullah pointed out in his report, one thing is clear: The mere fact that the villagers were willing to indict the army unit of conducting itself in such a despicable fashion revealed the depth of distrust of legally constituted authority.[10]

THE DISTRACTIONS OF THE GULF WAR

The Iraqi invasion and occupation of Kuwait in 1990 and the ensuing Gulf War had significant adverse consequences for India. Among other matters, the government had the unenviable task of organizing the airlift of over one hundred thousand stranded Indian workers in the Gulf states. Furthermore, the dramatically increased price of imported oil imposed severe costs on the Indian exchequer.[11] Faced with the tasks of coping with these unprece-

[9] See A. G. Noorani, "Exceeding the Brief: The Tragedy of the Verghese Report," *Frontline*, October 12–25, 1991, 107–9.

[10] Hamish McDonald, "Test of Honour," *Far Eastern Economic Review*, August 15, 1991, 24–6.

[11] Šumit Ganguly, "India Walks a Middle Path in Gulf Crisis," *Asian Wall Street Journal Weekly*, March 4, 1991.

dented setbacks, the government could not devote significant time and attention to the formulation of Kashmir policy. Furthermore, the weak minority government of Prime Minister Chandra Sekhar collapsed when the leader of the opposition, Rajiv Gandhi, on tenuous and personal grounds withdrew his support in early April.

Throughout 1991 the situation in Kashmir deteriorated. Foreign tourists were kidnapped, and in late April the government issued a directive asking all foreigners to leave the state. Furthermore, as the nation geared up for the Tenth General Election, no policy discussions were conducted on Kashmir. In effect, the Kashmir problem was handed over to bureaucrats in the Ministry of Home Affairs, to Governor Saxena in Kashmir, and to the Indian army and the paramilitary forces.

NARASIMHA RAO ENTERS

In late June 1991, following the assassination of Rajiv Gandhi on May 22 during the election campaign and a subsequent Congress(I) victory, Narasimha Rao, a former home affairs and foreign minister, assumed office as the new prime minister. The appointment of the new home affairs minister, S. B. Chavan, did little to improve the formulation of a new policy on Kashmir, however. The bulk of the energy of the new regime was consumed in preventing India's economic collapse in the wake of the Gulf War.[12] Later in the year, when the regime made some effort to start a dialogue with the insurgents, it quickly met with a firm rebuff from one of the principal insurgent organizations, the HUM, which refused to enter into any discussions with the government of India within the framework of the Indian Constitution.[13] In the meantime internecine differences continued to bedevil relations

[12] Sudeep Chakravarti, Zafar Agha, and Shahnaz Anklesaria Aiyar, "The Economy: Bold Gamble," *India Today,* July 31, 1991, 10–21.

[13] Agence France Presse Hong Kong, September 28, 1991, as reported in Foreign Broadcast Information Service, Near East and South Asia (FBIS-NES) 91-189, September 30, 1991.

between the HUM and the Jammu and Kashmir Liberation Front (JKLF).[14] Matters worsened when Yasin Malik, the leader of the JKLF, issued a public statement urging Pakistan to withdraw from "Azad Kashmir" to facilitate an overall settlement of the Kashmir dispute.[15]

Divisions also surfaced within the ranks of the government of India in early 1993. The minister of state for internal security, Rajesh Pilot, increasingly clashed with Chavan, the minister for home affairs. Pilot appeared more willing than his senior colleague to open channels of communication with the insurgents. Girish Saxena, the governor of Jammu and Kashmir, did not share Pilot's proclivity toward negotiation, however. Some commentators cast aspersions about Pilot's motivations for offering to negotiate with the insurgents. They contended that Pilot was inadequately informed about the prevailing political conditions within the state and was acting in haste in search of personal aggrandizement.[16]

On March 11, 1993, thanks to differences with Rajesh Pilot, Governor Girish Saxena was replaced by General Krishna Rao.[17] A senior retired Indian army officer, Lieutenant General M. A. Zaki, was made security adviser to the governor. Along with Zaki, Ashok Jaitley, a senior Indian Administrative Service officer with considerable experience and knowledge of Kashmir, was also appointed as an adviser to the governor. General Zaki, in turn, was put in charge of a Unified Command that sought to coordinate the activities of the Indian army as well as the paramilitary forces

---

[14] Syed Arif Bahar, "Reconciliation between Jammu-Kashmir Hizb-I al-Mujaheddin and Jammu-Kashmir Liberation Front," *Nawa-I-Waqt* (Urdu), October 24, 1992, 10.

[15] Agence France Presse Hong Kong, May 19, 1993, as reported in FBIS-NES-93-096, May 20, 1993.

[16] "Hasten Slowly in Kashmir," *Indian Express*, March 10, 1993, 8. See also Rita Manchanda, "Despite Much Talk, No Policy on Kashmir," *India Abroad*, June 4, 1993, 2–3.

[17] Binoo Joshi, "New Governor Is Ex-Army Chief," *India Abroad*, March 19, 1993, 12. Also see Manoj Joshi, "Policy of Drift," *Frontline*, May 21, 1993, 18–20, and Arun Joshi, "Militancy in J and K Assumes a New Dimension," *Hindustan Times*, May 17, 1993, 7.

operating in the valley. The Unified Command itself was composed of the additional chief secretary (home affairs), the divisional commissioner, the director-general of police, and the inspector-general of police for Kashmir.[18] Initially, the Unified Command was extremely effective. Later, it deteriorated into a mere coordinating agency, with the army calling the shots.

THE POLICE REVOLT

Barely a month and a half after his appointment as governor, General Krishna Rao confronted a crisis of significant proportions: a police revolt in Srinagar. The revolt, which involved as many as thirteen hundred policemen, laid siege to the police control room at the Batmaloo police station on April 27. The policemen were outraged over the death of a constable, Riaz Ahmed, in army custody on April 21. The constable had been arrested at the Hazratbal shrine on suspicion of links with the insurgents. On April 22, news of Ahmed's death spread throughout Srinagar, prompting a police strike.

Fearing an escalation of the tense situation at the police control room, the director-general of police, B. S. Bedi, called on the army for assistance. On April 28, three army battalions under the command of Brigadier Kshitin Pandya of the Eighth Mountain Division surrounded the police control room and forced the striking policemen to surrender. To the relief of many, the enterprise succeeded without a single shot being fired. Nevertheless, despite the success in disarming the rebel policemen and the appointment of a commission to investigate the death of the constable, resentment continued to resonate throughout the ranks of the state police.[19]

[18] Pravin Sawhney, "Army Operations in the Valley," *Indian Express,* August 16, 1993, 3.

[19] Binoo Joshi, "Troops Put Down Police Revolt," *India Abroad,* May 7, 1993, 6; Madhusudan Srinivas, "Bad to Worse," *Frontline,* May 21, 1993, 11–15; Sanjoy Hazarika, "Indian Army Troops Crush Revolt by Police in Kashmir," *New York Times,* April 29, 1993, A3.

THE HAZRATBAL INCIDENT

The governor's team did not manage to act with a similar degree of alacrity and skill when faced with the next major crisis in the state. In fact, the problems of coordination and control of the various armed units combating the insurgency were dramatized in mid-October 1993 when a group of insurgents successfully ensconced themselves in the famous Hazratbal mosque in Srinagar. The crisis began at about 6:30 on the evening of October 15 when G. M. Chisti, a member of the Muslim Auqaf Trust, informed a police constable, Ghulam Mohammed Shah, that several insurgents had entered the shrine and had tampered with the locks of the doors leading to the inner sanctum where the holy relic (the *moh-e-moqaddas* that was stolen and recovered in 1963) is kept. Shah, in turn, informed Inspector-General of Police Ashok Kumar Suri. Suri promptly alerted General Zaki. Zaki called a meeting of the Unified Command, where he stated that he had information that forty insurgents armed with light machine guns had moved into the Hazratbal shrine. He also said that he had information indicating that an attempt had been made to steal the holy relic. At the behest of the governor, Zaki ordered two Border Security Forces (BSF) companies to surround the mosque and block all entry and exit points. Some officials on the governor's staff were against laying the siege before verifying the particulars of the situation in the mosque. However, given the need for prompt action, they set aside their objections. Accordingly, a siege was laid around 10:00 P.M. Later, army units replaced the BSF companies around the mosque.

On October 17, Suri informed Divisional Commissioner Wajahat Habibullah that the insurgents who were inside the shrine wanted to speak to him. Habibullah held his initial conversations with the insurgents later that day. Contrary to press reports, General Krishna Rao gave Habibullah a free hand in negotiating with the insurgents. In the course of these negotiations, Habibullah obtained the services of two local religious notables, Maulvi Abbas

Ansari and Abdul Majeed Wani.[20] The combination of negotiations and the army siege proved successful. As part of the surrender agreement, the insurgents left their weaponry in the shrine. However, they refused to surrender to the army and insisted on the presence of the Jammu and Kashmir police.[21]

As in the case of the Kunan-Poshpora episode, providing an accurate reconstruction of the events during the Hazratbal crisis is difficult. Many of the press accounts were partial, and some were marked by political bias. They also tended to fabricate differences of opinion among the governor's staff. Contrary to press accounts, which also suggested fundamental differences on tactics and strategy between the governor and his civilian and military advisers, during the Hazratbal crisis they were mostly in accord.[22]

TALK ABOUT AN ELECTION

By the beginning of 1994, General Krishna Rao was increasingly an isolated figure in Srinagar. Following a near-fatal car accident, both General Zaki and Wajahat Habibullah had left their stations in Srinagar. And Ashok Jaitley, another key adviser, after a particularly frustrating effort to locate eighty-one missing persons, sought and was granted a transfer.[23]

At another level, India and Pakistan opened bilateral talks in January after a hiatus of more than a year. The discussions started on January 2, 1994, in Islamabad. The Indian delegation was led by J. N. Dixit, the Indian foreign secretary. The Pakistani delegation was headed by his counterpart, Shahrayar Khan. These talks,

---

[20] Personal correspondence with Wajahat Habibullah, minister for community affairs, Embassy of India, Washington, D.C., November 1995.

[21] Amit Baruah, "Advantage Nobody," *Hindu*, November 28, 1993, 4.

[22] Hamish McDonald, "Valley of Alienation," *Far Eastern Economic Review*, December 23, 1993, 20.

[23] Amitabh Mattoo, "Whose Victory Was It in Geneva Anyway?" *Independent* (New Delhi), March 14, 1994, 4. The "missing persons" are individuals who, it is widely believed in most quarters in Kashmir, have been picked up by the paramilitary forces under suspicion of collaboration with the insurgents.

which started on a positive note, quickly foundered as the differences over Kashmir proved Himalayan in size.

Around the time of these talks, to the surprise of both sides, the Chinese clearly indicated that they were firmly opposed to the emergence of an independent Kashmir. According to Pakistani sources, the Chinese were concerned that an independent Kashmir would become a hotbed of international intrigue directed at them and might call into question the territory Pakistan ceded to China in 1963.[24] Pakistan, nevertheless, sought to internationalize the Kashmir issue. Specifically, in March 1994 at the UN Human Rights Commission meeting in Geneva, it worked hard to pass a resolution condemning Indian human rights violations in Kashmir. Deft and concerted diplomacy enabled India to avoid such censure, but it entailed making common cause with such states as Iran and the People's Republic of China. Thoughtful political observers within India wondered aloud about this Pyrrhic victory.[25]

Amid these dispiriting political developments both within Kashmir and at the level of bilateral relations with Pakistan, some of Rajesh Pilot's advisers started to float the possibility of holding an election in Kashmir. The initial efforts to rekindle the political process through the promise of elections proved to be less than inspiring. Specifically, when Pilot visited Srinagar on March 26 accompanied by Farooq Abdullah, his motorcade came under fire near the Dal Gate area. Pilot, who was in a bulletproof car, escaped unhurt, as did Farooq.[26] Despite this setback, the government decided to press ahead with its plans for holding an election, in the absence of more creative measures.[27]

---

[24] Ahmed Rashid, "The China Factor," *Far Eastern Economic Review,* January 13, 1994, 12–13.

[25] Shekhar Gupta, "Triumph of Diplomacy," *India Today,* March 31, 1994, 26–33. For a measured assessment of the Indian success in blocking the Pakistani resolution in Geneva, see Malini Parthasarathy, "Facing the Realities in Kashmir," *Hindu,* March 14, 1994, 3.

[26] Binoo Joshi, "Rude Jolt for Political Initiative," *India Abroad,* April 8, 1994, 8.

[27] John F. Burns, "Rebels in Kashmir and Indian Army Ready for Long Fight," *New York Times,* May 16, 1994, 11–13.

To some extent the government's hopes of holding an election also stemmed from the war-weariness of the population of the state. Faced with harassment from both the insurgent groups and the security forces, most Kashmiris had started to yearn for relief from the continuing turmoil and violence.[28] This mood intensified in late July and early August after the assassination of Qazi Nissar Ahmad, a prominent religious figure in southern Kashmir. Though conclusive evidence may never be marshaled, it is widely believed that the HUM was behind his killing. Shortly before he was murdered, he had been acting as an intermediary between the Harkat-ul-Ansar insurgent group and authorities in Srinagar over the kidnapping of the son of David Housego, the former correspondent of the *Financial Times* in India.[29]

In an attempt to prepare the grounds for an election, the government released Yasin Malik, the leader of the JKLF, in early June. Large crowds showed up in Srinagar to greet Malik at his release. Malik initially expressed a willingness to hold talks with the government of India. However, the hostility of the HUM toward any discussions with the Indian government significantly reduced his room for maneuver.

Even as New Delhi started preparations for an election, critical observers within India warned about the dangers of holding an election that would garner little or no popular support. Some specifically warned the government not to make flawed inferences on the basis of the election that had brought the Beant Singh state government to power and had restored some normalcy to the Punjab since 1992. In the Punjab, unlike in Kashmir, the vast majority of the inhabitants did not feel fundamentally alienated from the Indian state. Furthermore, in the Punjab, even during the grimmest days of the insurgency, the basic institutional structures of the state still functioned. In Kashmir, for all practical purposes, the civil administration had collapsed.

[28] Rahul Bedi and Binoo Joshi, "New Hope for a Kashmir Solution," *India Abroad*, June 3, 1994, 20; Dipankar Banerjee, "Kashmir: A Change of Mood," *Frontline*, December 2, 1994, 38–40.

[29] Harinder Baweja, "The War Within," *India Today*, July 15, 1995, 32–3.

The government encountered other obstacles to holding elections. On October 17, Abdul Ghani Lone, a prominent member of the All-Party Hurriyat Conference (an agglomeration of various Kashmiri political parties—not including the National Conference—with ties to the insurgents), announced its decision to boycott the proposed poll. The Hurriyat's objections appeared to stem in large part from the belief that the government in New Delhi was attempting to promote Farooq Abdullah as the next chief minister of Kashmir.[30] Shabir Shah, a prominent young Kashmiri leader who had been incarcerated for advocating secession, also cast a shadow over the government's promise of holding elections. At his release from prison on October 14, Shah was greeted by a crowd of approximately two hundred thousand in Srinagar.[31] At this rally Shah publicly declared his opposition to the elections.[32] Abdul Ghani Lone and Syed Ali Shah Geelani, of the All-Party Hurriyat Conference, had expressed similar sentiments after being released from prison earlier in the year.

As the government continued with its preparations for holding the elections, the Chavan-Pilot feud continued unabated. Pilot insisted that some measure of autonomy should be granted to Jammu and Kashmir before the elections were held. Chavan, on the contrary, insisted on deferring any discussion of autonomy until after the elections. Matters reached a head in late October. Chavan, responding to a correspondent in London, indicated that Pilot's public statements on Kashmir could not be construed as official policy.[33] Prime Minister Narasimha Rao, who had long avoided a confrontation with Chavan, a trusted confidante and ally, finally stepped in to end this unseemly and increasingly public quarrel. Rao created a new Department of Jammu and Kashmir

[30] "Price of Indecision," *Statesman Weekly,* November 5, 1994, 9.
[31] Surinder Singh, " 'Jail Bird,' Shabir Shah to Be Released Today," *Mirror of Kashmir,* October 14, 1994, 1.
[32] Harinder Baweja, "Striking a New Resonance," *India Today,* November 15, 1995, 24–7.
[33] Hamish McDonald, "The Polls Ploy," *Far Eastern Economic Review,* November 17, 1994, 21.

Affairs in the prime minister's secretariat and made himself the minister in charge.[34]

LIGHTING THE FUSE AT CHARAR-E-SHARIEF

Rao's determination to hold elections in Kashmir not only engendered opposition from the insurgents and their supporters but also ran into institutional roadblocks. Two issues assumed particular salience. The 1991 census was not conducted in Jammu and Kashmir because of the unsettled political conditions in the state. As a consequence, constituencies could not properly be delimited for conducting elections. No delimitation had taken place since 1971. Furthermore, internal squabbles between the members of the Delimitation Commission and T. N. Seshan, the chief election commissioner, complicated matters.

At another level, the civil administrative machinery in the state had all but collapsed. Holding an election would entail drafting large numbers of state-level government employees for election and polling duties. Given the widespread demoralization and disaffection among the vast majority of government employees, it was unlikely that they would be of much use.[35]

As the government stumbled over these political, legal, and institutional roadblocks to an election, it suffered a dramatic setback. In May 1995, the Charar-e-Sharief shrine to the fourteenth-century Muslim cleric and Sufi saint Sheikh Nooruddin Noorani, near Srinagar, was burned. Like other events in the insurgency, the destruction of the shrine is virtually impossible to reconstruct with certainty. However, the key elements of the tragic episode can be reassembled. Some background information and analysis is in order to discuss the unfolding of the events that led up to the conflagration of May 11, 1995.

---

[34] Tarun Basu and Binoo Joshi, "Rao Takes Personal Charge of Affairs," *India Abroad*, November 11, 1994, 4.

[35] Sujay Gupta, "Valley Continues to Simmer in Anger after Five Years of President's Rule," *Statesman Weekly*, January 28, 1995, 6; A. G. Noorani, "Kashmir Polls: Legal and Political Snags," *Statesman Weekly*, June 18, 1994, 10.

Since 1992, following the collapse of the Najibullah regime in Afghanistan, Afghan *mujahideen* had started to emigrate into Kashmir. The prospects of fighting another *jihad* (holy war) had animated some. Others had been drawn by the prospects of mayhem and plunder. By 1995, reliable estimates placed their numbers around one thousand. Some operated with the HUM, while others joined similar pro-Pakistani groups such as al-Barq and al-Omar. The most powerful of the groups that emerged in 1993 following the consolidation of a number of smaller groups was the Harkat-ul-Ansar (Movement of the Companions of the Prophet).[36] Unlike the various Kashmiri insurgent groups, these organizations and their members proved to be especially vicious in their tactics and strategies. Lacking any blood-soil relationship with Kashmir, they were far more prone to engage in rapine and violence. Their lack of regard for the local population as well as their differences with other insurgent groups increasingly contributed to sanguinary and internecine battles.[37]

As early as February 1995, reports had emerged in the national media that a self-styled "major," Mast Gul, an insurgent of Afghan origin, had holed up near a mosque, the burial place of the Sufi saint in Charar-e-Sharief, along with some sixty to one hundred of his *condotierri*. The town of Charar-e-Sharief is twenty miles southwest of Srinagar. The security forces quickly moved to strengthen their deployments in and around the town, and a phase of psychological warfare ensued between them and the insurgents.[38] In an effort to wear down the insurgents in early March, the army cordoned off the town. In conjunction with the BSF contingents, they also started to regulate entry into the town. The insurgents, in turn, fortified the shrine with improvised explosive

---

[36] Anthony Davis, "The Conflict in Kashmir," *Jane's Intelligence Review* 7:1 (1995): 41–6.

[37] For an alternative formulation, which suggests that the presence of Afghans and other foreign mercenaries boosted the morale of the Kashmiri insurgents, see Rita Manchanda, "Who Is Afraid of Foreign Mercenaries?" *Pioneer,* September 2, 1993, 6.

[38] Sukumar Muralidharan, "A Shrine and a Siege," *Frontline,* April 21, 1995, 117–18. Also see Dinesh Kumar, "Stand-off at Charar-e-Sharief Is No Siege," *Times of India,* April 15, 1995, 6.

devices. Fearing that the insurgents might blow up the shrine, the security forces decided against a military operation designed to force them out of the shrine. Instead, around mid-March, the authorities offered safe passage to the insurgents, who repeatedly rebuffed this offer.[39] Over the course of the next two months the standoff continued. Occasionally, the two sides exchanged fire, with army snipers attempting to inflict serious casualties.

On May 8, quite abruptly, the insurgents set fire to a number of houses adjoining the shrine. It is widely surmised that this was an effort to escape by diverting the security forces. As the houses caught on fire, the army called in firefighters. However, owing to a constant stream of gunfire from the shrine and its immediate vicinity, the firefighters would not approach the fire. The ensuing blaze consumed the shrine and some one hundred adjoining homes and threatened four hundred other houses.[40] It is believed that during this melee, Mast Gul and some of his closest associates escaped. The army sought authorization from the prime minister's office to enter the town on May 9. It was eventually granted permission on May 11. Although Mast Gul had managed to slip through the cordon, the army captured Abu Jindal, the leader of the Harkat-ul-Ansar, during a cordon-and-search operation.

The burning of the shrine set off yet another round of protest in the valley, particularly as Abdul Ghani Lone of the Hurriyat Conference and Yasin Malik of the JKLF courted arrest on their way to Charar-e-Sharief. Most important, the government's plans for holding an election in Kashmir went up in the proverbial smoke. In the highly charged atmosphere that pervaded the state, the government could not seriously contemplate conducting an election in the foreseeable future.[41] The only positive development

---

[39] Ramesh Vinayak, "A Shocking Setback," *India Today,* May 31, 1995, 31–7.

[40] Molly Moore and John Ward Anderson, "Indian Forces, Rebels Fight in Kashmir," *Washington Post,* May 10, 1995, A30; John F. Burns, "In a Kashmir Conflagration, India Faces a Turning Point," *New York Times,* May 15, 1995, 12.

[41] Shiraz Sidhva, "Kashmir Peace Hopes Go Up in Smoke," *Financial Times,* May 15, 1995, 5.

that ensued in the wake of the destruction of the shrine was a signal from the prime minister's office that the government of India was willing to consider granting Kashmir a substantial degree of autonomy short of independence.[42] Yet the commitment to holding an election as a means of restoring political normality in the state remained the principal and preferred policy option available to the government in New Delhi, at least for the immediate term.[43]

The handling of the Charar-e-Sharief episode, from its start to its tragic end, revealed the lack of a clear-cut set of procedures and directives for dealing with such a crisis. Yet there was no lack of precedent. The government had faced similar situations in both the Punjab and Kashmir. After the calamity of "Operation Blue Star" in 1984 at the Golden Temple in Amritsar, the civilian authorities as well as the security forces displayed considerable skill and dexterity in the subsequent "Operation Black Thunder." In Kashmir, the government had also successfully defused the Hazratbal crisis despite initial missteps. What, then, explains the fiasco at Charar-e-Sharief? The blame cannot be placed on the tactics adopted by the army and the BSF.[44] Rather, civilian authorities in Srinagar and New Delhi were at fault. Having previously faced situations of siege, civilian authorities should have developed institutional mechanisms and standard operating procedures to defuse them. Unfortunately, given New Delhi's distraction with other issues and the idiosyncratic and reactive decision making on Kashmir, they had not promoted the development of such measures. In the absence of clear-cut political choices and robust institutional mechanisms for formulating and implementing a coherent policy toward the larger crisis in Kashmir, the tragedy at Charar-e-Sharief was all but inevitable.

[42] John F. Burns, "Indian Prime Minister Hints at Concessions to Kashmir Muslims," *New York Times,* May 18, 1995, A15.

[43] Bishakha De Sarkar, "CHARARRED," *Telegraph,* May 21, 1995, 9.

[44] M. L. Thapan, "CHRAR-E-SHARIF: Lessons from Past Failures," *Statesman,* May 2, 1995, 4.

CONCLUSIONS

The civil war in Kashmir has followed a desultory course for the better part of a decade. It is highly unlikely that the insurgents can prevail on the battlefield or can effectively obtain the intervention of the international community. India's staying power on the ground in Kashmir is inestimable. The Indian state has historically fought and successfully fended off previous challenges to its integrity even at a time when it possessed significantly less coercive power. The continued sanguinary conflict in Kashmir may indeed be extremely corrosive to the ethos of the Indian army, not to mention the paramilitary forces. Nevertheless, apart from an "attentive public" that cares deeply about these matters, public opinion in India does not appear overly exercised about the state's Kashmir policy.[45] Furthermore, the opinions of those in the Indian attentive public are hardly monolithic. Many have only minor reservations about the government's Kashmir policy. Some, in fact, believe that the government has not responded with sufficient vigor in dealing with the insurgents or their principal supporter, Pakistan.[46]

Yet India will not concede Kashmir, for a number of compelling reasons. First, virtually all Indians consider Kashmir to be part of India. The Kashmiri insurgent claim of national self-determination, if allowed to prevail, could lead to the disintegration of the Indian state. The demonstration effects of Kashmir seceding from India would be profound. Second, in a related fashion, the secession of Kashmir would unwittingly implicate the

[45] The evidence for this assertion is largely impressionistic. It is based on a number of conversations with policy makers, academics, and journalists in New Delhi and other Indian metropolitan centers. The term "attentive public" is derived from the work of Gabriel Almond, *The American People and Foreign Policy* (New York: Praeger, 1960), 151. The term refers to individuals who are knowledgeable about and interested in public affairs.

[46] See, for example, Ravi Rikhye, "Time to Tell U.S. that the Two-Nation Theory Is Out," *India Abroad*, November 3, 1995, 2.

remaining Muslim population in India. Intellectually, this argument is untenable. Indian Muslims should under no circumstances have to answer for the behavior of their religious brethren in Kashmir. It is nonetheless a tragic fact of present-day Indian political life. Any national government that ignores this would do so at its own peril. Third, the insurgent claim for self-determination is itself problematic. The vast majority of the insurgents would not extend the privilege of self-determination to members of other communities. Despite the many malfeasances of the Indian state, the best hope for the redressal of the grievances of all minorities remains within the ambit of a secular, democratic, and federal Indian polity.

It is not entirely clear whether the militants will succeed in drawing the attention of the international community to coerce India into fundamentally altering its policies in Kashmir. Pakistan has routinely raised the Kashmir issue at various UN forums since 1990. These efforts, though obviously an irritant for India, have not made a meaningful difference to Indian policy making.[47] Given India's unhappy experience with the Kashmir issue at the United Nations, it is doubtful that India will allow the issue to be internationalized.[48] At best, persistent international criticism of India's human rights record in Kashmir has led to greater sensitivity to the issue and some effort at reform of paramilitary operations and procedures. It has also prompted the Indian government to pass an ordinance creating the National Human Rights Commission in 1993. (In 1994, legislation was passed to give the ordinance the force of law.)

To restore order as well as law, India will have to undertake a thorough reexamination of its policies in Kashmir. A small step in that direction was taken between May and September 1966, when

[47] Ela Dutt, "Bhutto Lashed Out at India over Kashmir," *India Abroad,* November 3, 1995, 10.

[48] The Indian experience at the United Nations is nicely summarized in Jyoti Bhusan Das Gupta, *Jammu and Kashmir* (The Hague: Martinus Nijhoff, 1968).

the government of India held both parliamentary and state assembly election in Jammu and Kashmir. Both elections resulted in extraordinarily high voter turnout. Allegations of official misconduct marred the parliamentary elections, however. A number of Indian newsmagazines charged that the security forces had coerced significant sections of the populace to vote. The news media lodged few, if any, such grievances against the conduct of the state assembly elections. The conditions under which both elections were held and the prospects for normality are discussed in the epilogue to this book.

7

Strategies and options for resolving the crisis

Various strategies and options have been suggested for the resolution of the crisis in Kashmir. The spectrum ranges from coercively altering the demographic profile of the state to conceding independence and sovereignty. Ultimately, the resolution of the insurgency in Kashmir will not conform to any preconceived blueprint.[1] It will eventually be resolved through a combination of force, negotiation, and compromise among the contending parties. From the principal options that have been discussed and considered, however, it is possible to delineate some of the key components of any potential settlement.

ETHNIC FLOODING

One option, which has been only partially articulated, is "ethnic flooding."[2] This strategy would involve altering the demographic profile of the valley by encouraging large numbers of Hindus to

---

[1] For a discussion of various blueprints (and their critiques) for the resolution of the Kashmir problem, see Robert G. Wirsing, *India, Pakistan, and the Kashmir Dispute: On Regional Conflict and Its Resolution* (New York: St. Martin's, 1994).

[2] This term emerged during the course of a conversation with Professor Kanti Bajpai, School of International Studies, Jawaharlal Nehru University, New Delhi, January 1994.

131

move into the Kashmir valley.[3] It is believed that the transformation of the demography of the valley would simultaneously profoundly change its political coloration. Since the newly introduced population would be fiercely loyal to the Indian state, it is supposed, the issue of secession would be rendered moot.

A first step toward this end would be to repeal Article 370 of the Indian Constitution. This article, which has a number of provisions, prohibits the sale of immovable property to non-Kashmiris; in effect, it prevents non-Kashmiris from permanently settling in the state.[4] This stipulation was included in the Indian Constitution in recognition of the unique circumstances of Kashmir's accession to India in 1947.

Once this legal barrier is removed, large numbers of Indian citizens from other parts of India would be encouraged to settle in the valley. Over time such a population transfer would dramatically transform the valley into a predominantly Hindu region. Implicit in this argument is the belief that the Muslims in the valley are disloyal to India and that Hindu migrants from other parts of India would pledge their allegiance to the Indian state for its having allowed their migration in the first place.

This strategy is not unlike the policy that the Labor government pursued in the Israeli-occupied West Bank after the 1967 war. In another parallel with the Israeli settlement process, the Indian government would have to augment substantially its police and paramilitary presence in order to ensure the safety and security of

[3] Professor Amitabh Mattoo of the School of International Studies, Jawaharlal Nehru University, has pointed out that right-wing Hindu jingoists have realized the difficulty of flooding the valley with Hindus, given its predominantly Muslim population. Instead they are now arguing that Ladakh and Jammu be settled with Hindus. If a plebiscite were held, all three provinces would be included and thereby affect its final outcome. Personal communication, March 28, 1996.

[4] On this point, see Chitta Basu, "Abrogating Article 370 Can Only Bring More Disaster," and Dinesh Gupta, "A Case against Article 370," in *Secular Crown on Fire: The Kashmir Problem,* ed. Asghar Ali Engineer (New Delhi: Ajanta, 1991). The text of Article 370 can be found in Appendix 2 of this book.

these newly arrived migrants. It would also have to increase public spending in the state, for two reasons: to meet the enlarged demand for a range of public services, including schools, hospitals, housing, and roads; and to boost the economy of the state to create new sources of employment.[5]

This strategy would be highly unlikely to succeed. Surprisingly, the legal barrier would in all likelihood be the easiest to breach. Apart from India's "attentive public," many Indians do not seem to comprehend fully the significance of Article 370. If a Bharatiya Janata Party–dominated national government came to power, it might well be able to muster the necessary votes to abrogate Article 370.

The other components of the strategy would be far more difficult to implement. At the present time, after the flight of some 250,000 Hindus from the valley, the population of Kashmir is composed almost entirely of Muslims. Transforming the demographic profile of Kashmir would require an enormous Hindu migration. Ensuring the safety and security of migrants in a region racked by an insurgency is a task well beyond the capabilities of the Indian state. Currently, the paramilitary units and the Indian army are stretched to a breaking point.[6] Furthermore, the Indian exchequer would be hardpressed to generate the resources necessary to meet the sharply increased demands for infrastructural and employment projects. The strategy of ethnic flooding, although it may be superficially attractive and laden with populist appeal, is fundamentally unworkable.

THE MAILED-FIST STRATEGY

Another approach, which also commands a degree of populist appeal, can be referred to as the "mailed-fist" strategy. Again, this

---

[5] For an excellent discussion of the Israeli strategy, see Ian S. Lustick, *Unsettled States, Disputed Lands: Britain and Ireland, France and Algeria, Israel and the West Bank–Gaza* (Ithaca, N.Y.: Cornell University Press, 1993).

[6] Author interview with Indian journalist, New Delhi, August 1995.

option has not yet been explicitly articulated.[7] This strategy would involve markedly increasing the military pressure that is currently being applied in the state. The singular goal of this approach would be to crush the insurgents militarily. No quarter would be given to the insurgents in pursuit of this strategy.

In popular parlance, this approach is called "doing another Punjab." Under the leadership of K. P. S. Gill, a senior Indian police officer from the Assam cadre, the insurgents in the Punjab were defeated through the ruthless and unbridled application of force.[8] With the insurgents on the run, elections were held, initially at the state and subsequently at the local level. The state elections of 1992, which followed five years of insurgency and direct rule from New Delhi, resulted in extremely low voter turnouts but did bring to power a legally constituted government. The subsequent local elections produced extraordinarily high turnouts—more than 80 percent of the eligible electorate. Widespread coercion appeared to have produced the necessary conditions for peace.[9]

A similar strategy has been proposed for handling the insurgency in Kashmir. But this option is as deeply flawed as the preceding one. First, the demographic composition of Kashmir is markedly different from that of the Punjab. In the Punjab, the Sikh population barely outnumbered the Hindu population,[10] whereas Kashmir has a clear Muslim majority. More to the point, the vast

---

[7] This option can be inferred, however, from the work of a former governor of Jammu and Kashmir, Jagmohan Malhotra, *My Frozen Turbulence in Kashmir* (New Delhi: Allied, 1991).

[8] On this point, see Steve Coll, *On the Grand Trunk Road* (New York: Random House, 1994), chapter 9.

[9] The seeming end of the insurgency was called into question with the dramatic assassination of Chief Minister Beant Singh in front of the government secretariat in Chandigarh on September 2, 1995. Beant Singh had come to power in the Punjab in 1992. See Clarence Fernandez, "Indian Police Suspects Inside Job in Punjab Killing," Reuters wire report, September 3, 1995.

[10] On this point, see the discussion in M. J. Akbar, *India: The Siege Within* (New Delhi: Penguin, 1987).

majority of the Sikhs in the Punjab did not support the creation of a separate state of Khalistan, even after the 1984 pogroms in New Delhi and elsewhere and even though they were deeply disaffected from the Indian government. In the Kashmir valley, the seat of the insurgency, the vast majority of the population is already alienated from the Indian state. Consequently, it is unlikely that the "hearts and minds" of the Kashmiris could be won over as easily after unleashing a harsh counterinsurgency campaign.

Second, the political status of the territory of Kashmir is an important factor. Kashmir has been the subject of a territorial dispute between India and Pakistan almost since the moment the two countries were created. Despite Pakistani support for various Khalistani terrorist groups, Pakistan never had any claims on the Punjab. Consequently, the government of India did not have to prosecute a two-pronged strategy. It could systematically apply force with a considerable degree of impunity. On the Kashmir issue, however, Pakistan can raise the question of human rights violations, and it has done so. In response, India has been forced to snuggle up to such curious political bedfellows as Iran and the People's Republic of China (PRC) to fend off international disapprobation.

Third, part of the Indian government's strategy in the Punjab was to seal the border with barbed wire, trenches, floodlights, and machine-gun towers, making the entire state virtually impenetrable. The success of a counterinsurgency strategy depends in large part on the ability of government forces to deny the insurgents sanctuary and sources of material support. Sealing the Punjab border created conditions conducive to the implementation of such an approach.[11] A similar tactic would be all but impossible in Kashmir because the terrain does not permit it. Kashmir's physical proximity to Pakistan, coupled with its highly mountainous territory, makes creating a cordon sanitaire around the valley exceedingly difficult.

---

[11] Author interview with former senior official in the Ministry of Home Affairs, New Delhi, January 1993.

Fourth, the international community is now far more consistently focused on human rights violations. Between 1993 and 1995, India has taken important steps to limit the likelihood of human rights violations. International pressure and scrutiny led to the creation of the National Human Rights Commission in 1993 and also to a "human rights cell" in the Indian Army.[12] Returning to an unbridled counterinsurgency strategy would inevitably undermine the fitful progress that the Indian government has made in protecting human rights in those very counterinsurgency situations. This strategy would also bring overwhelming pressure from a variety of international quarters for India to rein in its security forces.

Fifth and finally, the pursuit of a no-holds-barred strategy would have a profoundly corrosive impact on the ethos and morale of the Indian army. In the 1990s, senior army officers, including one chief of staff of the Indian army, expressed serious reservations about the repeated involvement of the army in "aid-to-the civil" operations.[13] The pursuit of a full-scale counterinsurgency operation would inevitably involve the Indian Army and would place some of its units in untenable situations.

THE WEAR-DOWN OPTION

The current strategy that the government of India is pursuing in Kashmir reflects years of institutional learning from the counterinsurgency operations that the government conducted in India's northeastern region during the 1960s and the 1970s. In the northeast, India's strategy was to wear down the fighting spirit of the

[12] Indian army officials are loath to discuss publicly the scope and activities of the "human rights cell." An officer with the rank of colonel heads up the cell. Among other matters, the cell is responsible for drawing up a human-rights curriculum for officers serving in counterinsurgency situations. (Author interview with senior Indian army official, New Delhi, January 1995).

[13] Rahul Bedi, "Concern on Army's Internal Use," *India Abroad*, February 26, 1993, 5.

insurgents over an extended period of time.[14] This strategy involved the extensive use of force and, in the view of some Indian human rights activists, included significant violations of human rights. Two factors led to the collapse of those insurgencies. First, after fighting the Indian army and paramilitary forces for over two decades, the insurgents realized that the Indian government forces would eventually prevail. Furthermore, the insurgents' principal supporter, the PRC, lost its desire to foment rebellion abroad and, at the same time, wanted to improve relations with India. Consequently, the insurgents' major source of support was cut off. Today, even though the northeast is hardly trouble-free, many of the leaders of that insurgency are prominent politicians. Along with the British experience in Malaysia and the Philippine government's success against the Hukbalahap rebellion, India's experience in the northeast counts as one of the few genuinely successful examples of counterinsurgency operations.[15] It is hardly surprising, then, that some Indian governmental agencies have inferred that this model can be applied with equal vigor elsewhere.

Nevertheless, there are fundamental contextual differences between the northeastern experience and the Kashmir situation. First, like the Punjab, the northeastern areas of India were not disputed territories. The rebels in the northeast did make appeals to international forums, but these appeals were largely ignored. Their foreign supporters, other than the PRC, were few and far between. Consequently, the government of India could, without the slightest hesitation, insist that the problem was an internal one. Even though the government has adopted the same posture on Kashmir, segments of the international community tend to see the Kashmir problem as a bilateral dispute between India and Pakistan.

---

[14] On this point, see Onkar Marwah, "New Delhi Confronts the Insurgents," *Orbis* 21:1 (1977): 353–73.

[15] For a thoughtful critique of counterinsurgency doctrines in general and American models in particular, see Michael D. Schafer, *Deadly Paradigms: The Failure of U.S. Counterinsurgency Strategy* (Princeton: Princeton University Press, 1988).

Second, the sheer physical isolation of the northeastern areas removed the actions of the insurgency and the government's counterinsurgency measures from public scrutiny both in India and abroad. Kashmir, on the other hand, has commanded both domestic and international attention from the very outset. The government paramilitary forces, in large part because of the pressures of international and domestic scrutiny, cannot act with impunity.

Third, as a consequence of deft Indian diplomacy and the loss of the PRC's revolutionary fervor, the steady supply of weaponry to the northeastern rebels tapered off by the late 1970s, gradually giving the government forces a decided advantage. In Kashmir, however, despite India's concerted efforts to implicate Pakistan in aiding the rebels, there has been no appreciable decline in the quality or quantity of weaponry available to the insurgents. Furthermore, the Kashmiri rebels appear to have access to the floating arms bazaar that was spawned in South-Central Asia at the end of the Afghan war.[16]

Fourth, in the northeast there were specific individuals and groups that the government of India could seek out as negotiating partners. Unfortunately, in Kashmir the fragmented nature of the insurgency makes it exceedingly difficult to pinpoint viable negotiators. As many as 130 insurgent groups currently operate in the valley. (See Appendix 5.) Furthermore, even the two principal groups, the Jammu and Kashmir Liberation Front (JKLF) and the Hizb-ul-Mujahideen (HUM), have engaged in internecine warfare. It is also by no means clear that the Hurriyat Conference, a loose agglomeration of some thirty political parties, can negotiate on behalf of the insurgents.

Fifth, despite assertions to the contrary in India, such a long-term strategy is fraught with at least the *possibility* of inadvertent escalation. It is true that all three Indo-Pakistani wars resulted from deliberate, conscious decisions. Nevertheless, Pakistan's decision to resort to war in 1965 was profoundly influenced by a

[16] Selig Harrison and Geoffrey Kemp, *India and America after the Cold War* (Washington, D.C.: Carnegie Endowment for International Peace, 1993).

series of cognitive and affective misperceptions.[17] It would not be inconceivable for similar misperceptions to provoke another international conflict. Although both the Indian and the Pakistani forces have shown considerable restraint along the Line of Control (LOC) in Kashmir, such restraint can break down from the cumulative effects of stress, miscalculation, and misperception.[18] Some evidence already exists that a spiral of mutual misunderstandings brought India and Pakistan close to another full-scale war in 1990.[19]

Despite all these caveats, it should nevertheless be conceded that a wear-down strategy may well work over the long haul. The staying power of the Indian state is considerable. After several years, the insurgents could be worn down and their numbers reduced. Furthermore, Pakistan may also tire of supporting the insurgents. There is already growing resentment among Kashmiris against the presence and harsh tactics of the opportunistic Afghan *mujahideen* who have entered the fray. Furthermore, the pristine quality of the movement has to a very large extent been lost. Many of the Kashmiri insurgent groups are interested solely in engaging in mayhem, extortion, and kidnapping.[20] The criminalization of significant portions of the movement has denuded the insurgents' base of support among the local population. The government of India could profit from this growing sentiment against the insurgents. At some point in the future, a war-weary and violence-fatigued population may

---

[17] For the origins of the Indo-Pakistani conflicts, see Šumit Ganguly, *The Origins of War in South Asia: The Indo-Pakistani Conflicts since 1947*, 2d ed. (Boulder: Westview, 1994). For a discussion of the role of misperceptions in the Indo-Pakistani war of 1965, see Šumit Ganguly, "Deterrence Failure Revisited: The Indo-Pakistani War of 1965," *Journal of Strategic Studies* 13:4 (December 1990): 77–93.

[18] After the 1971 war and the Simla Agreement of 1972, the Cease-Fire Line in Jammu and Kashmir was converted into the Line of Control; it is the de facto international border between Indian-held Kashmir and Pakistani-held Kashmir.

[19] Seymour Hersh, "On the Nuclear Edge," *New Yorker*, March 29, 1993, 56–73.

[20] Harinder Baweja, "The Hostage Crisis," *India Today*, September 15, 1995, 19–25.

decide that making a deal with New Delhi and ending the routin-
ized violence is preferable to the status quo.

CONCEDING THE VALLEY

Appalled at the continuing carnage in Kashmir and concerned
about the corrosive effect on the Indian Army and the paramilitary
forces, a small coterie of individuals in New Delhi have suggested
that it may be best for India to declare victory and simply concede
the valley to Pakistan. This proposal has seemingly intuitive appeal. It would enable India to retain control of Jammu, Kargil, and
Leh while simultaneously addressing a number of concerns. It
would bring an end to the insurgency, enable the Indian Army and
paramilitary forces to withdraw from an untenable situation, and
satisfy Pakistan's irredentist claim to the Kashmir valley.

The apparent simplicity of this proposal masks a range of problems, however. First, no government in New Delhi, at least in the
foreseeable future, will be able to muster the political support
necessary to pursue this option. Despite the enormous human and
material costs that New Delhi has incurred in Kashmir, conceding
the valley to its principal adversary is politically indefensible. Any
government that seriously entertained this proposal would be writing its own death warrant. In effect, this option fails the important
test of political feasibility.

Even if it were politically feasible, this option would fall short
on a number of other counts. Conceding the valley to Pakistan
might not satisfy all the insurgent groups, some of which, most
notably the JKLF, remain committed to the notion of a unified,
independent Kashmir. It is also unclear that conceding the valley
would satisfy all of Pakistan's ambitions. Having obtained the
valley, Pakistan might simply revive its claim to the entire princely
state of Jammu and Kashmir, barring the portions that it conceded
to China in 1963. Furthermore, Pakistan might construe India's
concession as a sign of India's weakness and pusillanimity; just
such a misinterpretation led to war in 1965.

In addition, the government of India might well be loath to

make such a bold territorial concession for fear of demonstration effects. India is still engaged in delicate negotiations with the PRC on a long-standing border dispute. A willingness to concede the valley to Pakistan under duress could have extremely deleterious consequences in India's negotiations with the PRC.

Furthermore, conceding the valley would leave the northern portions of the state, the districts of Leh and Kargil, far more vulnerable militarily; they would remain connected to Jammu by a narrow neck of land that could easily be severed in a wartime situation. Indian military planners who still rue the concession of the strategic Haji Pir Pass after the 1965 war with Pakistan would find this territorial concession simply intolerable.

Finally, by conceding the valley, India would be abandoning its moral commitments to a significant portion of its own citizenry—Hindus, Buddhists, and even Muslims who have little desire to become Pakistani citizens. In effect, this option would completely negate the rights of minorities within minorities.

SHARED SOVEREIGNTY

Yet another seemingly creative option, that of shared sovereignty, has been suggested. This strategy, though not spelled out with great clarity or precision, proposes that Kashmir become a condominium between India and Pakistan. The two sides would jointly administer the state of Jammu and Kashmir, with Kashmiris able to move freely across a porous border.[21]

Any attempt to implement this proposal would encounter a

---

[21] Variants of this proposal can be found in the writings of Hamish McDonald, Ayesha Jalal, B. G. Verghese, and Joseph E. Schwartzberg. See, for example, Hamish McDonald, "Forced into a Corner," *Far Eastern Economic Review,* December 23, 1993, 18–20; Ayesha Jalal, "Kashmir Scars," *New Republic,* July 23, 1993; B. G. Verghese, "The Fourth Option," *Hindustan Times,* March 25, 1993, 4; and Joseph E. Schwartzberg, "An American Perspective II," *Asian Affairs* 22:1 (Spring 1995): 71–87. Schwartzberg offers the most detailed blueprint. Among other matters, he spells out the conditions for the creation of a Kashmir Autonomous Region (KAR). The problems discussed herein remain nevertheless.

plethora of political and administrative obstacles, however. Would India and Pakistan share sovereignty over all of Kashmir's affairs or only in the area of defense? Would Kashmir be self-governing in all areas except defense and external security? Who would be responsible for maintaining civil order in the face of disturbances? If India and Pakistan were jointly responsible, how would they mediate the inevitable differences over their responsibilities? Who would be allowed to emigrate to and settle in a jointly held Kashmir? On what basis would settlement be permitted? Who would be responsible for the collection of revenue? Who would assume responsibility for economic development? Finally, and perhaps most important, why would Pakistan accept this as a desirable solution? The seemingly endless list of logistical hurdles indicates the practical futility of this option.

HOLDING A PLEBISCITE

It is always possible to return to a plebiscite as a possible means of settling the dispute. The UN Security Council resolution of April 21, 1948, called for Pakistan's withdrawal of its "nationals" from Kashmir and the subsequent holding of a plebiscite. A second resolution, passed on August 13, 1948, took into account the presence of Pakistani troops in Kashmir, which, according to the wording of the resolution, constituted "a material change in the situation." This resolution called for Pakistan to withdraw its troops in order to produce conditions conducive to holding a plebiscite.[22] Various arrangements for holding a plebiscite were also contained in subsequent UN resolutions.

But would a plebiscite yield a fair and just solution to the problem? A number of compelling arguments can be made against a plebiscite.[23] First, the very terms of the plebiscite would be

---

[22] The tortured history of the UN-sponsored attempts to broker a peace in Kashmir is nicely covered in Jyoti Bhusan Das Gupta, *Jammu and Kashmir* (The Hague: Martinus Nijhoff, 1968).

[23] The extraordinary logistical difficulties of holding a plebiscite are discussed in Lawrence T. Farley, *Plebiscites and Sovereignty* (Boulder: Westview, 1986).

sharply contested. The government of Pakistan would insist that the options in any plebiscite be limited to two: a choice between joining India or joining Pakistan. Pakistan would insist that the so-called third option—independence—be ruled out. The PRC, which came to occupy a significant portion of Jammu and Kashmir after the 1962 border war, has also categorically ruled out the option of independence. Some Kashmiris, however, would insist that the independence option be part of any plebiscite.

Second, if the majority of Kashmiris did vote for independence, what guarantees would be made to the minority Hindu and Buddhist populations of the state? As Amitai Etzioni has cogently argued, plebiscites and other strategies of self-determination in the postcolonial age do very little to address the rights of minorities within minorities.[24] In the Kashmir case many of the groups demanding the right of self-determination on the basis of their minority status would be quite loath to extend the same principle to others in their midst. Some harbingers of their future behavior are already apparent: The vast majority of the insurgent groups, the HUM in particular, have repeatedly threatened and even attacked a number of journalists and newspaper offices to quell adverse reporting.[25]

INDEPENDENCE

Yet another option that merits discussion is one that was introduced above: independence. The JKLF, one of the oldest and very possibly the most popular secessionist organization, notionally favors independence. As indicated in the preceding section, however, this option faces a number of structural hurdles. Remarkably, the three regional powers that have important stakes in the conflict—India, Pakistan, and China—all agree that independence as an option will *not* be countenanced. The reasons for the Indian

---

[24] Amitai Etzioni, "The Evils of Self-Determination," *Foreign Policy* 89 (Winter 1992–3): 21–35.

[25] Vikram Parekh, *On a Razor's Edge* (New York: Committee to Protect Journalists, 1995).

and Pakistani opposition to the creation of an independent state of Kashmir are clear; both sides fear the demonstration effect that such a territorial loss could have on their respective polities. Interestingly enough, the costs of Kashmir's independence would, in all likelihood, be far worse for Pakistan. Granting independence to "Azad Kashmir" could ring the death knell of the Pakistani state. The Chinese remain adamantly opposed to the independence of Kashmir for similar, if not identical, reasons. They fear that an independent Kashmir would provide a tremendous boost to the hopes and demands for Tibet's independence. The Chinese also believe that an independent Kashmir could be used to conduct intrigues against them in the twenty-first century.[26]

Finally, the best-financed and most powerful secessionist organization, the HUM, remains firmly opposed to independence. Its posture is hardly surprising; the bulk of its financial, logistical, and moral support comes from Pakistan.

THE PROTECTORATE OPTION

A particularly innovative and bold option for settling the insurgency has recently been suggested: the "protectorate option."[27] This strategy entails turning the Kashmir valley, the principal locus of the insurgency, into an Indian protectorate. According to this proposal, the government in the valley, under a treaty arrangement with India, would be able to control all domestic and external policy issues except that of defense. This would go well beyond returning the valley to its pre-1952 status (in which it controlled all but defense, foreign affairs, and communications). Simultaneously, the government in the valley would have to agree to five critical terms: a guarantee of minority rights, the continued secular status of the region, the maintenance of democratic representative

---

[26] Ahmed Rashid, "The China Factor," *Far Eastern Economic Review,* January 13, 1994, 12–13.

[27] This option was suggested to me by Professor Amitabh Mattoo of the School of International Studies, Jawaharlal Nehru University (personal communication, March 28, 1996).

institutions, the safe return of Kashmiri Hindus to the valley and the restoration of their property, and a demobilization of all militant groups in the valley. The districts of Leh, and Kargil, and Jammu would be made into Union Territories.

This strategy meets the demands of the various Kashmiri insurgent groups to a very large extent. Although this arrangement falls short of the independence that some of the insurgents are demanding, it grants the Kashmir valley an unparalleled degree of autonomy. Through its insistence on the return of the Hindus to the valley, it also addresses right-wing sentiment within India. Finally, it effectively removes Pakistan from any discussion of the settlement of the dispute.

Despite the obvious advantages of this arrangement, it has some potential shortcomings. How would a semi-independent Kashmir valley ensure its own economic viability? Would India have to subsidize it? How would India subsidize it? What legal rights would Kashmiris have in the rest of India? What would be the basis of citizenship? This option would present difficult administrative hurdles for both the Indian state and the Kashmiri leadership. Finally, would a semi-independent Kashmir be able to contend with an unrequited Pakistan across the border?

AN ALTERNATIVE STRATEGY

What, then, constitutes a workable strategy for bringing an end to the insurgency? Any option that fails to recognize the fundamental territorial integrity of India will not meet the test of political feasibility. No government in India will concede Kashmir, even if it entails continuing losses in blood and treasure, for two reasons. First, most, if not all, of India's national leaders believe that the secession of Kashmir would set off centrifugal forces throughout the country. Furthermore, many within India's attentive public also hold that the secession of India's only Muslim-majority state could have profoundly deleterious consequences for the rest of the country's Muslim population, who might find themselves punished for the secession of Kashmir. Such a possibility cannot be dis-

missed as a mere chimera. Given the rise and increasing respect-
ability of fanatical Hindu sentiment in India, such a scenario must
be considered plausible.

Second, the Indian state has demonstrated considerable resil-
ience in handling insurgencies. Even today its coercive power remains considerable. In the absence of a viable alternative strategy,
the Indian state can and will continue to use substantial force to
curb the insurgency, domestic and international criticism notwithstanding.

The current strategy may have reached its structural limits,
however. The status quo in Kashmir amounts to a stalemate;
neither side can win outright. If the conflict continues in its present
form, both sides will continue to pay an exceedingly high price.
Of course, given the greater firepower, resources, and tenacity of
the Indian state, it will eventually prevail, simply by wearing out
the insurgents. But this would amount to a Pyrrhic victory. More
than a generation of Kashmiris would remain sullen and deeply
alienated from the Indian state. Indian rule in Kashmir would
have tenuous political legitimacy and would be subject to periodic
challenges. Finally, apart from the material costs of continuing, the
price of this insurgency could include the long-term moral effect
on the Indian forces. A prolonged, brutal counterinsurgency operation could corrode morale and probity within the army and the
paramilitary units.

Yet this bleak future should hardly be deemed inevitable. A
change of politico-military strategy, even at this late stage, can
ward off such an outcome. One possible alternative strategy
should be considered. On the international front, the United States
should be persuaded to pressure Pakistan to stop supporting the
insurgents. Pakistan's support of the insurgency is critical; the
insurgents derive sanctuary, weaponry, and logistical support from
Pakistan. In return for American pressure on Pakistan to cease
support for the insurgents, India should undertake a number of
steps to restore both law and order in Kashmir. Second, negotiations should be initiated with Pakistan. After years of unrelenting
violence in Kashmir, Pakistan is no closer to realizing its goal of

wresting Kashmir away from India. It has been more successful in pursuing its secondary objective: raising the cost (to India) of the Indian presence in Kashmir. This result, contrary to Pakistani assertions, is fraught with considerable risk. On at least one occasion since the beginning of the insurgency in 1989, India and Pakistan have come precipitously close to full-scale war.[28] The two could reach such a point again, or war could actually break out, through a combination of misperception and inadvertence.[29] Consequently, it is in the interests of both sides to resume bilateral negotiations. In these negotiations, India could offer Pakistan a package of concessions. This package could build on the six non-papers that were offered to Pakistan in January 1994.[30] Specifically, India could offer to make unilateral concessions in three areas of contention: Sir Creek, the Wullar Barrage, and the Siachen Glacier.[31] Additionally, it could offer Pakistan limited territorial concessions along the LOC in Kashmir. These concessions could repeat the offer that Sardar Swaran Singh made to Zulfiquar Ali Bhutto in 1963, during a series of bilateral talks on the subject of Kashmir.

Within Kashmir, India will have to negotiate with the insurgents. The Indian government, to its credit, has already started this process. In 1994 it released two of the principal leaders of the JKLF, Yasin Malik and Shabir Shah. Subsequently, in 1996 the government initiated negotiations with some former leaders of various insurgent groups.[32] The next step in this process may

[28] Devin T. Hagerty, "The Theory and Practice of Nuclear Deterrence in South Asia" (Ph.D. diss., University of Pennsylvania, 1995).

[29] Devin T. Hagerty, "South Asia's Nuclear Balance," *Current History* 95:600 (April 1996): 165–70.

[30] "Non-papers Presented by India during Indo-Pakistani Foreign Secretary–Level Talks in January 1994," Embassy of India, Washington, D.C.

[31] A. G. Noorani, *Easing the Indo-Pakistani Dialogue on Kashmir: Confidence-Building Measures for the Siachen Glacier, Sir Creek, and the Wular Barrage Disputes,* Occasional Paper no. 16 (Washington, D.C.: Henry L. Stimson Center, 1994).

[32] In February 1996, the minister for home affairs, S. B. Chavan, held talks in New Delhi with four former insurgent leaders—Babbar Badr of the Muslim Janbaz Force, Bilal Lodhi of the al-Barq, Ghulam Mohiuddin

prove to be difficult, but it is nevertheless necessary: The Indian government must offer a time-bound cease-fire arrangement. Once the principal groups have agreed to a cease-fire, the government can continue negotiations with representatives from the insurgent movement.

What would be the subject of these negotiations? Neither independence nor a merger with Pakistan is a viable option. Short of those two options, the government of India can offer the insurgents significant concessions in the immediate and long terms. In the short term, as a means of building trust and confidence, the government can offer an unconditional amnesty to the insurgents. Such a proposal will not be easy to sustain politically. Certain political groups, most prominently the BJP, will vigorously oppose any such move. The Indian army and the paramilitary forces, which have suffered significant casualties, will also strenuously object.[33] Nevertheless, in the interests of waging peace in Kashmir, the government will have to demonstrate a degree of boldness. It could also offer to mete out condign punishment to members of the armed forces who have exceeded their orders.[34] The government has already taken some initial steps in that direction. It could go further, however, by providing greater information on the cases it has prosecuted and the punishments handed down.

Over the longer term, once a cease-fire has been established, the government could offer to make several key concessions to the

Lone of the Muslim Mujahideen, and Imran Rahi of the Hizb-ul-Mujahideen—about holding elections in Jammu and Kashmir. See Jawed Naqvi, "New Delhi Holds Talks with Militants in Kashmir but Mainstream Militants Stay Out," *India Monitor,* March 24, 1996, 4. Also see Harinder Baweja, "Peace Bombshell," *India Today,* February 29, 1996, 46–7.

[33] For a sample of the objections, see the responses to Šumit Ganguly, "Conflict Resolution in South Asia: An American Perspective," in *The Road Ahead: Indo-U.S. Strategic Dialogue,* ed. Jasjit Singh (New Delhi: Lancers, 1994).

[34] For a discussion of the abuse of authority by the various paramilitary forces, see Paula R. Newberg, *Double Betrayal: Repression and Insurgency in Kashmir* (Washington, D.C.: Carnegie Endowment for International Peace, 1995), 25–30.

militants. First, since many of the grievances in Kashmir are related to electoral irregularities, the government could suggest holding the next election under international auspices. Neutral observers could be present to ensure that no electoral shenanigans take place. The Indian national Election Commission—which has, in the recent past, shown increasing signs of assertiveness—should welcome the possibility of demonstrating such transparency.[35] Second, the government could offer two longer-term concessions. It could return Kashmir to its pre-1952 status, when the central government in New Delhi controlled only defense, foreign affairs, and communications. The government could also allow the Kashmiris to write their own constitution, for a second time. Such a constitutional dispensation could bolster various institutional arrangements within Jammu and Kashmir. It could strengthen existing judicial bodies and electoral procedures and alter recruitment practices into administrative agencies. Such efforts would contribute significantly toward improving institutional procedures at the state and local levels. Improving the functional efficacy and capabilities of such organizations is critical for responding to the needs of a highly mobilized population. It needs to be underscored that the erosion of such institutional arrangements contributed to the insurgency.

These proposals hardly amount to a complete panacea for the Kashmir conundrum. Nevertheless, they offer a politically realistic approach to a vexing issue that has shown few signs of going away. Indeed, it is entirely possible that even this package of concessions and bilateral negotiations with Pakistan will not address the demands of certain insurgent groups. Faced with further intransigence, the government of India would have little choice but to use force to subdue those groups unwilling to negotiate. Furthermore, it is entirely likely that Pakistan will not fully abandon its irredentist claim to Kashmir, even if it accepts the package of unilateral concessions. However, if this strategy could succeed

[35] Charu Lata Joshi, "Starting the Countdown," *India Today,* January 31, 1996, 26–29.

in securing an end to active Pakistani support for the insurgency, in turn giving the Indian government leverage to begin outright negotiations with the insurgent groups, that would be reason enough to grant Pakistan some concessions.

Epilogue

In 1996, the government of India launched a two-pronged strategy in an attempt to restore a degree of political normality to the violence-ridden Kashmir valley. The first part of the strategy involved opening negotiations with a group of insurgents who had recently been released from long-term incarceration in Indian prisons. The home minister, S. B. Chavan, along with Home Secretary K. Padmanabhiah, initiated these talks in February 1996. Babbar Badr of the Muslim Janbaz Force, Imran Rahi of the Hizb-ul-Mujahideen (HUM), Bilal Lodhi of the Hurriyat Conference, and Ghulam Mohiuddin Lone of the Muslim Mujahideen all agreed to hold unconditional talks with the government of India. Ahsan Dar, a still-imprisoned HUM leader, quickly endorsed the decision of his colleagues. Once the negotiations were under way, the insurgents indicated a willingness to continue their discussions with the government despite their refusal to participate in the forthcoming Lok Sabha (parliamentary) elections.[1]

Even as the government was preparing the logistics of the understandably complicated elections in Kashmir, the violence continued. One of the more serious episodes took place at the beleaguered Hazratbal shrine in Srinagar. On March 24, 1996, members of a breakaway faction of the Jammu and Kashmir Liberation Front (JKLF) forced their way into the shrine. In marked contrast to the approach the government had adopted toward the seizure of the shrine in 1993, on this occasion the

---

[1] Harinder Baweja, "Peace Bombshell," *India Today*, February 29, 1996, 46–7; Tarun Basu and Binoo Joshi, "Ground-Breaking Talks with Militants," *India Abroad*, March 22, 1996, 6; Sheikh Mushtaq, "Kashmir Militant Groups Reject Poll Plans but Continue to Talk with Government Representatives," *India Monitor*, March 31, 1996, 17.

government showed little quarter; the state governor, retired general Krishna Rao, adopted a tough confrontational stance. In a gun battle that broke out between the insurgents and members of the Border Security Force (BSF), some thirty insurgents were killed.[2]

Despite such continued violence, the government pressed ahead with its plans to implement the second prong of its strategy—to hold parliamentary elections in Jammu and Kashmir. These elections were held between May 7 and May 30, 1996, in conjunction with the nationwide Eleventh General Election in India. Congress(I) candidates won four of the six parliamentary seats: Ghulam Mohammad Mir won in Srinagar; Ghulam Rasool Kar, in Baramulla; Mangat Ram Sharma, in Jammu; and P. Namgyal, in Ladakh. The seats in Anantnag and Udhampur were won by a Janata Dal candidate, Mohammad Maqbool Dar, and the Bharatiya Janata Party's state president, Chaman Lal Gupta, respectively.[3] The turnout in these elections was dramatically higher than in the 1989 parliamentary elections. In the 1989 elections, voter turnout was around 2 percent.[4] In the 1996 elections, turnout was nearly 40 percent.[5] Widespread allegations charged that voter coercion by the BSF and the Rashtriya Rifles was partially responsible for this high turnout.[6]

Before the elections, the central government, in a bid to undermine the various insurgent groups, created several counterinsur-

---

[2] Sheikh Mushtaq, "Troops Seal Off Kashmir's Holiest Shrine after a Fierce Gun Battle," *India Monitor,* March 31, 1996, 1; Binoo Joshi, "30 Guerillas Killed in Hazratbal Gun Battles," *India Abroad,* April 5, 1996, 12. For an especially critical account of the government's handling of the crisis, see Praveen Swami, "An Encounter at Hazratbal," *Frontline,* June 14, 1996, 121.

[3] Binoo Joshi, "Congress Party Is the Unexpected Winner," *India Abroad,* June 7, 1996, 7.

[4] Harinder Baweja, "Exercise in Opportunism," *India Today,* April 30, 1996, 70–1.

[5] Ajith Pillai, "Vote Marshalled," *Outlook,* June 5, 1996, 10–15.

[6] Shiraz Sidhva, "Guns and Votes," *Frontline,* June 14, 1996, 122–5.

gent movements, the most prominent of which is the Ikhwan-e-Muslimoon. This organization, under the leadership of Kukka Parray, a former insurgent leader, was provided with weapons, money, and protection by the government.[7] In addition to attacking insurgent groups, the Ikhwan-e-Muslimoon created a political wing, the Awami League, and contested the elections. To their surprise and dismay, both the Awami League candidates— Javed Ahmed Shah and Ghulam Nabi Mir, from Srinagar and Baramulla, respectively—lost.[8]

Despite the record turnout in these elections, the government moved only marginally closer to restoring normality to the politics of Kashmir. The use of coercive tactics to ensure a high voter turnout may well have been counterproductive. Admittedly, the extent and degree of coercion involved in these elections are subject to debate.[9] The government's assertion that without large-scale security and some pressure on the electorate the election might not have taken place cannot be dismissed. All the major insurgent groups had threatened to thwart the elections. Many of them did attempt, albeit largely unsuccessfully, to disrupt the electoral process.[10] They also issued explicit warnings to the editors of local newspapers not to publish information pertaining to the elections.

Nevertheless, the use of the security forces to induce voters to participate in these elections has hurt the national government's attempt to restore political legitimacy in Kashmir. In the catalytic 1987 assembly elections, which in many ways helped precipitate the insurgency, the Congress(I) and National Conference workers

---

[7] Harinder Baweja and Ramesh Vinayak, "A Dangerous Liaison," *India Today,* March 15, 1996, 52–5; also see Human Rights Watch/Asia, "India's Secret Army in Kashmir: New Patterns of Abuse Emerge in the Conflict," *Human Rights Watch/Asia Report* 8:4 (May 1996).

[8] Binoo Joshi, "Counterinsurgents Angry at Voting Setback," *India Abroad,* June 14, 1995, 16.

[9] Praveen Swami, "A Surprise in Kashmir: The Myth of Coercion at Large," *Frontline,* June 14, 1996, 114–20.

[10] Binoo Joshi, "Voter Turnout Seen as Anti-separatist," *India Abroad,* May 31, 1996, 14.

had overwhelmed polling agents to ensure a Congress(I)–National Conference victory. In the 1996 elections, although the security forces did not attempt to direct voters toward any particular party or candidate, their overbearing behavior raised profound questions about the fairness of the elections. Although the government claimed an initial victory against the insurgents, its reputation for probity and the sincerity of its commitment to the democratic process remain tarnished, both among the residents of the valley and in the view of outside observers.[11]

The Indian government, with no clear mandate after the fractious results of the 1996 elections nationwide, faces both a challenge and an opportunity in Kashmir. Its challenge is to restore trust and confidence in the central government after years of malfeasances by prior administrations. Yet an unprecedented opportunity may also be on the horizon. Despite the intransigence of most of the insurgent groups, many of the inhabitants of the valley may view this government favorably simply because it is not complicit in the malfeasances of the past. One of the first initiatives of the United Front government under Prime Minister Deve Gowda called for a re-examination of center-state relations and the retention of Article 370.[12]

In a determined effort to bring some semblance of normality to the Kashmir valley the government of India held elections for the state assembly between September 7 and 30, 1996. The government was able to conduct elections in the state because a distinct sense of war weariness had set in among a significant segment of the population of the valley.[13] The earlier Lok Sabha elections of May–June 1996 had been characterized by widespread allegations of voter coercion. The conduct of the September elections, by

[11] Ajith Pillai, "Setback for 'Renegades,' " *Outlook,* June 12, 1996, 18–19.

[12] United Front, "A Common Approach to Major Policy Matters and a Minimum Programme" (June 5, 1996), as reprinted in *Mainstream,* June 15, 1996, 13–20.

[13] Binoo Joshi, "Hope for Normalcy Mounts as Polling Begins," *India Abroad,* September 6, 1996. p. 4.

contrast, did not lead to any charges of voter intimidation or official misconduct.[14] The only notes of dissent came from entirely expected quarters: The Hurriyat Conference dismissed the electoral results and vowed to continue its struggle for "self-determination," [15] and Prime Minister Benazir Bhutto of Pakistan declared the elections a "sham" and accused India of attempting to divert international attention.[16]

The National Conference under the leadership of Farooq Abdullah won a decisive victory in the state, obtaining 57 of a possible 87 seats. In the valley, the National Conference won 40 of a possible 44 seats. On October 8, Farooq Abdullah was sworn in as the chief minister. Soon after assuming office Abdullah announced the formation of a 27-member council of ministers.

The tasks before this new government are daunting. To begin with, the government will have to restore some semblance of a rule of law in the troubled state. The new government has already shown a willingness to take steps in that direction. On October 11, Farooq Abdullah announced that his regime would set up a human-rights commission to look into allegations of human-rights violations.[17] Pursuit of this goal will not be easy. The government will face stiff opposition from the higher echelons of the security forces, who will argue vigorously against any such probes. Nevertheless, to win back the trust and confidence of the Kashmiris in the valley, such efforts to repair the fractured rule of law are essential. The government also faces the unenviable prospect of disarming and rehabilitating the counterinsurgent groups that the security forces had created from the ranks of former insurgents. Although precise

---

[14] Inderjit Badhwar, "A New Beginning," *India Today,* September 30, 1996, pp. 26–31.
[15] "Pro-India Party in Kashmir Wins a Landslide Victory in Elections," *New York Times,* October 3, 1996, p. A6.
[16] Nirmal Mitra, "Bhutto Calls Election Sham, Cites Indian Papers," *India Abroad,* October 11, 1996, p. 8.
[17] "Commission to Probe Human Rights Abuses," *India Abroad,* October 18, 1996, p. 18.

numbers are unavailable, it is widely believed that close to five thousand counterinsurgents are still operating in the valley.[18]

The new regime will also have to maintain pressure on the various insurgent groups. Despite the success of the elections, the insurgency is far from over. Battle-hardened insurgents continue to stalk the valley. Violence is still commonplace. Unless these groups and their leaders evince a willingness to negotiate an end to the insurgency, the new government will have no option but to continue military operations against them.

Finally, the government will have to start negotiations with the Hurriyat Conference. Although it refused to take part in the electoral process, and consequently it lacks any institutional standing in Kashmiri politics, the Hurriyat represents a segment of radical opinion. As long as it remains outside the ambit of normal electoral politics, it will continue to undermine efforts to quell the civil war.

[18] Harinder Baweja and Ramesh Vinayak, "Farooq in the Forefront," *India Today,* September 30, 1996, pp. 33–42.

Appendix 1

The Instrument of Accession of Jammu and Kashmir State (October 26, 1947)

Whereas, the Indian Independence Act, 1947, provides that as from the fifteenth day of August 1947, there shall be set up an independent Dominion known as India, and that the Government of India Act, 1935, shall, with such omissions, additions, adaptations and modifications as the Governor-General may by order specify, be applicable to the Dominion of India;

And whereas the Government of India Act, 1935, as so adapted by the Governor-General provides that an Indian State may accede to the Dominion of India by an Instrument of Accession executed by the Ruler thereof;

Now, therefore,

I, Shriman Indar Mahandar Rajrajeshwar Maharajadhiraj Shri Hari Singhji, Jammu Kashmir Naresh Tatha Tibbet adi Deshadhipathi, Ruler of Jammu and Kashmir State, in the exercise of my sovereignty in and over my said State Do hereby execute this my Instrument of Accession and

1. I hereby declare that I accede to the Dominion of India with the intent that the Governor-General of India, the Dominion Legislature, the Federal Court and any other Dominion authority established for purposes of the Dominion shall, by virtue of this my Instrument of Accession, but subject always to the terms thereof, and for the purposes only of the Dominion, exercise in relation of the State of Jammu and Kashmir (hereinafter referred

157

to as "this State") such functions as may be vested in them by or under the Government of India Act, 1935, as in force in the Dominion of India on the 15th day of August 1947 (which Act as so in force is hereafter referred to as "the Act").

2. I hereby assume the obligation of ensuring that due effect is given to the provisions of the Act within this State so far as they are applicable therein by virtue of this my Instrument of Accession.

3. I accept the matters specified in the Schedule hereto as the matters with respect to which the Dominion Legislature may make laws for this State.

4. I hereby declare that I accede to the Dominion of India on the assurance that if an agreement is made between the Governor-General and the Ruler of this State whereby any functions in relation to the administration in this State of any law of the Dominion Legislature shall be exercised by the Ruler of this State, then any such agreement shall be deemed to form part of this Instrument and shall be construed and have effect accordingly.

5. The terms of this my Instrument of Accession shall not be varied by any amendment of the Act or of the Indian Independence Act, 1947, unless such amendment is accepted by me by [in] an Instrument supplementary to this Instrument.

6. Nothing in this Instrument shall empower the Dominion Legislature to Make any law for this State authorising the compulsory acquisition of land for any purpose, but I hereby undertake that should the Dominion for the purposes of a Dominion law which applies in this State deem it necessary to acquire any land, I will at their request acquire the land at their expense or if the land belongs to me transfer it to them on such terms as may be agreed, or, in default of agreement, determined by an arbitrator to be appointed by the Chief Justice of India.

7. Nothing in this Instrument shall be deemed to commit me in any way to acceptance of any future constitution of India or to fetter my discretion to enter into arrangements with the Government of India under any such future constitution.

8. Nothing in this Instrument affects the continuance of my sovereignty in and over this State, or, save as provided by or under

this Instrument, the exercise of any powers, authority and rights now enjoyed by me as Ruler of this State or the validity of any law at present in force in this State.

9. I hereby declare that I execute this Instrument on behalf of this State and that any reference in this Instrument to me or to the Ruler of the State is to be construed as including a reference to my heirs and successors.

Given under my hand this twenty-sixth day of October, nineteen hundred and forty-seven.

HARI SINGH

Maharajadhiraj of Jammu and Kashmir State

Appendix 2

Article 370 of the Indian Constitution (1950)

370[1] (Temporary provision with respect to the State of Jammu and Kashmir)—

(1) Notwithstanding anything in this Constitution,—

(a) the provision of article 238 shall not apply in relation to the State of Jammu and Kashmir;

(b) the power of Parliament to make laws for the said State shall be limited to—

(i) those matters in the Union List and the Concurrent List which, in consultation with the Government of the State, are declared by the President to correspond to matters specified in the Instrument of Accession governing the accession of the State to the Dominion of India as the matters with respect to which the Dominion Legislature may make laws for that State; and

---

[1] In exercise of the powers conferred by this article the President, on the recommendation of the Constituent Assembly of the State of Jammu and Kashmir, declared that, as from the 17th day of November, 1952, the said art. 370 shall be operative with the modification that for the Explanation cl. (1) thereof, the following Explanation is substituted namely:

"Explanation: For the purpose of this article, the Government of the State means the person for that time being recognized by the President on the recommendation of the Legislative Assembly of the State as the Sadar-i-Riyasat of Jammu and Kashmir, acting on the advice of the Council of Ministers of the State for the time being in office."

(ii) such other matters in the said Lists, as, with the concurrence of the Government of the State, the President may by order specify.

Explanation—For the purposes of this article, the Government of the State means the person for the time being recognized by the President as the Maharaja of Jammu and Kashmir acting on the advice of the Council of Ministers for the time being in office under the Maharaja's Proclamation dated the fifth day of March, 1948;

(c) the provisions of article 1 and of this article shall apply in relation to that State;

(d) such of the other provisions of this Constitution shall apply in relation to that State subject to such exceptions and modifications as the President may by order² specify:

Provided that no such order which relates to the matter specified in the Instrument of Accession of the State referred to in paragraph (i) of sub-clause (b) shall be issued except in consultation with the Government of the State:

Provided further that no such order which relates to matters other than those referred in the last preceding proviso shall be issued except with the concurrence of that Government.

(2) If the concurrence of the Government of the State referred to in paragraph (ii) of sub-clause (b) of clause (1) or in the second proviso to sub-clause (d) of that clause be given before the Constituent Assembly for the purpose of framing the Constitution of the State is convened, it shall be placed before such Assembly for such decision as it may take thereon.

(3) Notwithstanding anything in the foregoing provision of this article, the President may, by public notification, declare that this

---

² See the Constitution (Application to Jammu and Kashmir) Order, 1954 (C.O. 48) as amended from time to time in Appendix I [of the Indian Constitution].

article shall cease to be operative or shall be operative only with such exceptions and modifications and from such date as he may specify:

Provided that the recommendation of the Constituent Assembly of the State referred to in clause (2) shall be necessary before the President issues such a notification.

Appendix 3

The Tashkent Agreement (January 10, 1966)

The Prime Minister of India and the President of Pakistan, having met at Tashkent and having discussed the existing relations between India and Pakistan, hereby declare their firm resolve to restore normal and peaceful relations between their countries and to promote understanding and friendly relations between their peoples. They consider the attainment of these objectives of vital importance for the welfare of the 600 million people of India and Pakistan.

(I) The Prime Minister of India and the President of Pakistan agree that both sides will exert all efforts to create good neighborly relations between India and Pakistan in accordance with the United Nations Charter. They reaffirm their obligation under the Charter not to have recourse to force and to settle their disputes through peaceful means.

They considered that the interests of peace in their region and particularly in the Indo-Pakistani sub-continent and, indeed, the interests of the peoples of India and Pakistan were not served by the continuance of tension between the two countries. It was against this background that Jammu & Kashmir was discussed, and each of the sides set forth its respective position.

TROOPS WITHDRAWAL

(II) The Prime Minister of India and the President of Pakistan have agreed that all armed personnel of the two countries shall be withdrawn not later than February 25, 1966, to the position they held prior to August 5, 1965, and both sides shall observe the cease-fire terms of the cease-fire line.

(III) The Prime Minister of India and the President of Pakistan have agreed that relations between India and Pakistan shall be based on the principle of non-interference in the internal affairs of each other.

(IV) The Prime Minister of India and the President of Pakistan have agreed that both sides will discourage any propaganda directed against the other country, and will encourage propaganda which promotes the development of friendly relations between the two countries.

(V) The Prime Minister of India and the President of Pakistan have agreed that the High Commissioner of India to Pakistan and the High Commissioner of Pakistan to India will return to their posts and that the normal functioning of diplomatic missions of both countries will be restored. Both Governments shall observe the Vienna Convention of 1961 on diplomatic intercourse.

TRADE RELATIONS

(VI) The Prime Minister of India and the President of Pakistan have agreed to consider measures towards the restoration of economic and trade relations, communications, as well as cultural exchanges between India and Pakistan, and to take measures to implement the existing agreements between India and Pakistan.

(VII) The Prime Minister of India and the President of Pakistan have agreed that they give instructions to their respective authorities to carry out the repatriation of the prisoners of war.

(VIII) The Prime Minister of India and the President of Pakistan have agreed that both sides will continue the discussions of questions relating to the problems of refugees and eviction of illegal immigration. They also agreed that both sides will create conditions which prevent the exodus of people. They further agreed to discuss the return of the property and assets taken over by either side in connection with the conflict.

SOVIET LEADERS THANKED

(IX) The Prime Minister of India and the President of Pakistan have agreed that both sides will continue meetings both at the highest and at other levels on matters of direct concern to both countries. Both sides have recognized the need to set up joint Indo-Pakistani bodies which will report to their Governments in order to decide what further steps should be taken.

(X) The Prime Minister of India and the President of Pakistan record their feelings of deep appreciation and gratitude to the leaders of the Soviet Union, the Soviet Government and personally to the Chairman of the Council of Ministers of the USSR for their constructive, friendly and noble part in bringing about the present meeting which has resulted in mutually satisfactory results. They also express to the Government and friendly people of Uzbekistan their sincere thankfulness for their overwhelming reception and generous hospitality. They invite the Chairman of the Council of Ministers of the USSR to witness this declaration.

Appendix 4

The Simla Agreement (July 2, 1972)

The Government of Pakistan and the Government of India are resolved that the two countries put an end to the conflict and confrontation that have hitherto marred their relations and work for the promotion of a friendly and harmonious relationship and the establishment of durable peace in the subcontinent, so that both countries may henceforth devote their resources and energies to the pressing task of advancing the welfare of their peoples.

In order to achieve this objective, the Government of Pakistan and the Government of India have agreed as follows:

i) That the principles and purposes of the Charter of the United Nations shall govern the relations between the two countries;

ii) That the two countries are resolved to settle their differences by peaceful means through bilateral negotiations or by any other peaceful means mutually agreed upon between them. Pending the final settlement of any of the problems between the two countries, neither side shall unilaterally alter the situation and both shall prevent organization, assistance and encouragement of any acts detrimental to the maintenance of peaceful and harmonious relations;

iii) That the prerequisite for reconciliation, good neighborliness and durable peace between them is a commitment by both the countries to peaceful co-existence, respect for each other's territorial integrity and sovereignty and non-interference in each other's internal affairs, on the basis of equality and mutual benefit;

iv) That the basic issues and causes of conflict which have bedeviled the relations between the two countries for the last 25 years shall be resolved by peaceful means;

v) That they shall always respect each other's national unity, territorial integrity, political independence and sovereign equality;

vi) That in accordance with the charter of the United Nations they will refrain from the threat or use of force against the territorial integrity or political independence of each other.

Both Governments will take all steps within their power to prevent hostile propaganda directed against each other. Both countries will encourage the dissemination of such information as would promote the development of friendly relations between them.

In order progressively to restore and normalize relations between the two countries step by step, it was agreed that:

i) Steps shall be taken to resume communications, postal, telegraphic, sea, land including border posts, and air links including overflights.

ii) Appropriate steps shall be taken to promote travel facilities for the nationals of the other country.

iii) Trade and cooperation in economic and other agreed fields will be resumed as far as possible.

iv) Exchange in the fields of science and culture will be promoted.

In this connection delegations from the two countries will meet from time to time to work out the necessary details.

In order to initiate the process of the establishment of durable peace, both the Governments agree that:

i) Pakistani and Indian forces shall be withdrawn to their side of the international border.

ii) In Jammu and Kashmir, the Line of Control resulting from the ceasefire of December 17, 1971, shall be respected by both sides without prejudice to the recognized position of either side. Neither side shall seek to alter it unilaterally irrespective of mutual differences and legal interpretations. Both sides further undertake to refrain from threat or the use of force in violation of this Line.

iii) The withdrawals shall commence upon entry into force of this agreement and shall be completed within a period of 30 days thereof.

This agreement will be subject to ratification by both countries in accordance with their respective constitutional procedures, and will come into force with effect from the date on which the instruments of ratification are exchanged.

Both Governments agree that their respective Heads will meet again at a mutually convenient time in the future and that, in the meanwhile, the representatives of the two sides will meet to discuss further the modalities and arrangements for the establishment of durable peace and normalisation of relations, including the question of repatriation of prisoners of war and civilian internees, a final settlement of Jammu and Kashmir and the resumption of diplomatic relations.

ZULFIKAR ALI BHUTTO
President, Islamic Republic of Pakistan

INDIRA GANDHI
Prime Minister, Republic of India

Simla, the 2nd July, 1972

Appendix 5

The principal Kashmiri insurgent groups:
A profile

Al-Jehad The militant wing of the People's League, this group is based largely in the Anantnag district. Though it remains active, its members are both disorganized and undisciplined.

Al-Omar This organization was the militant wing of the Awami Action Committee. Its support base was located in the Jami Masjid/ Rajouri Kadal area of downtown Srinagar. Since the arrest of its leader, Mushtaq Latram, in 1993, the organization has lost much of its earlier strength. Its political objectives, beyond extortion, are unclear.

Allah Tigers This group has "Azad Kashmiri" origins, is pro-Pakistani in orientation, and has ties to the Hizb-i-Islami of Afghanistan. It was active in the early phase of the insurgency but has now been confined to the periphery.

Harkat-ul-Ansar This group, which was implicated in the destruction of Sheikh Nooruddin Noorani's (Nand Rishi) shrine in May 1995, is pro-Pakistani in orientation. One of its principal leaders, the self-styled "Major" Mast Gul, escaped to Pakistan after the confrontation with the Indian security forces at Charar-e-Sharief. Estimates of its strength are placed between 750 and 1,000. A significant number of its cadres are Afghans.

Hizbollah   This pro-Pakistani group was active in the Batmaloo area of Srinagar. Since the arrest and incarceration of its leader, Mushtaq-ul-Islam, in 1991, this group's activities have declined.

Hizb-ul-Mujahideen (HUM)   This is the largest and best-armed insurgent group in Kashmir. It emerged in early 1990. The HUM issued threats to the Kashmiri pandits and played a vital role in ensuring their exodus from the valley. It is the militant wing of the Jammat-i-Islami-i-Kashmir. One estimate places its active membership around 4,000. A large number of its cadres are foreigners, principally Afghans. Its initial leader was Master Ahsan Dar, who is currently incarcerated. Its present leader is Salahuddin (a nom de plume). Salahuddin had been a candidate for the assembly election from Lal Chowk. The HUM is widely considered to be pro-Pakistani and seeks to create an Islamic republic in Kashmir.

Ikhwanul Muslimeen   This organization was responsible for a spate of kidnappings between 1990 and 1992. Among its victims were Naheed Soz, the daughter of Saifuddin Soz, a member of Parliament; Doraiswamy, a director of the Indian Oil Corporation; and Dr. and Mrs. Wakhloo, a former principal of the Regional Engineering College and his wife, a former minister in G. M. Shah's government. This organization is pro-Pakistani in orientation.

Jammu and Kashmir Liberation Front (JKLF)   This is the oldest and arguably the most popular of the various insurgent groups. It was founded in the United Kingdom in June 1976 by Amanullah Khan and Maqbool Butt. The organization traces its lineage to the Kashmir National Liberation Front, which was founded by Amanullah, Butt, and Hashim Qureshi in the late 1960s. The JKLF is notionally secular and supports the creation of an independent Kashmir. The JKLF (Valley) is an appendage of the parent organization and ostensibly shares the former's ideological orientation. In late 1995 the JKLF (Valley) gave up its underground status and nominally joined the Hurriyat Conference. This transformation was made possible by the release of Yasin Malik, a prominent JKLF leader, from government of India custody in 1994. Malik has abjured violence and has concentrated on civil disobedience. The JKLF (Valley) was responsible for the kidnapping of Dr. Rubaiya Sayeed in 1989 and was the vanguard of the insurgency from 1989 to 1991. One of its more notorious members, Bitta Karate, was responsible for a series of murders in 1990 including that of the Srinagar Doordarshan (state-run television) chief Lassa Kaul. Karate is now in prison.

Lashkar-e-Tolba This is one of the smaller insurgent groups, composed mostly of Afghans and Pakistanis. It has been active since 1994.

Sources: Personal interviews, Washington, D.C., September 1990 and May 1996; personal interviews, Ministry of Home Affairs, New Delhi, January 1995; Harinder Baweja, "Who's Who of Militancy," *India Today*, September 15, 1995, 24; Philip E. Jones, "Paradise Lost: The Revolt in Kashmir," South Asia Division, Office of Near East and South Asia Analysis, Central Intelligence Agency, Washington, D.C., 1990 (photocopy).

Index